MADMEN
ON THE COUCH

MADMEN ON THE COUCH

Analyzing the Minds of the Men and Women of the Hit TV Show

Dr. Stephanie Newman

Thomas Dunne Books
St. Martin's Griffin
New York

THOMAS DUNNE BOOKS.
An imprint of St. Martin's Press.

www.thomasdunnebooks.com
www.stmartins.com

Library of Congress Cataloging-in-Publication Data

Newman, Stephanie, Dr.
Mad men on the couch : analyzing the minds of the men and women of the hit tv show / Stephanie Newman.—1st ed.
p. cm.
ISBN 978-1-250-00298-3 (trade pbk.)
ISBN 978-1-250-01443-6 (e-book)
1. Mad men (Television program) I. Title.
PN1992.77.M226N49 2012
791.45'72—dc23

2011045152

First Edition: February 2012

10 9 8 7 6 5 4 3 2 1

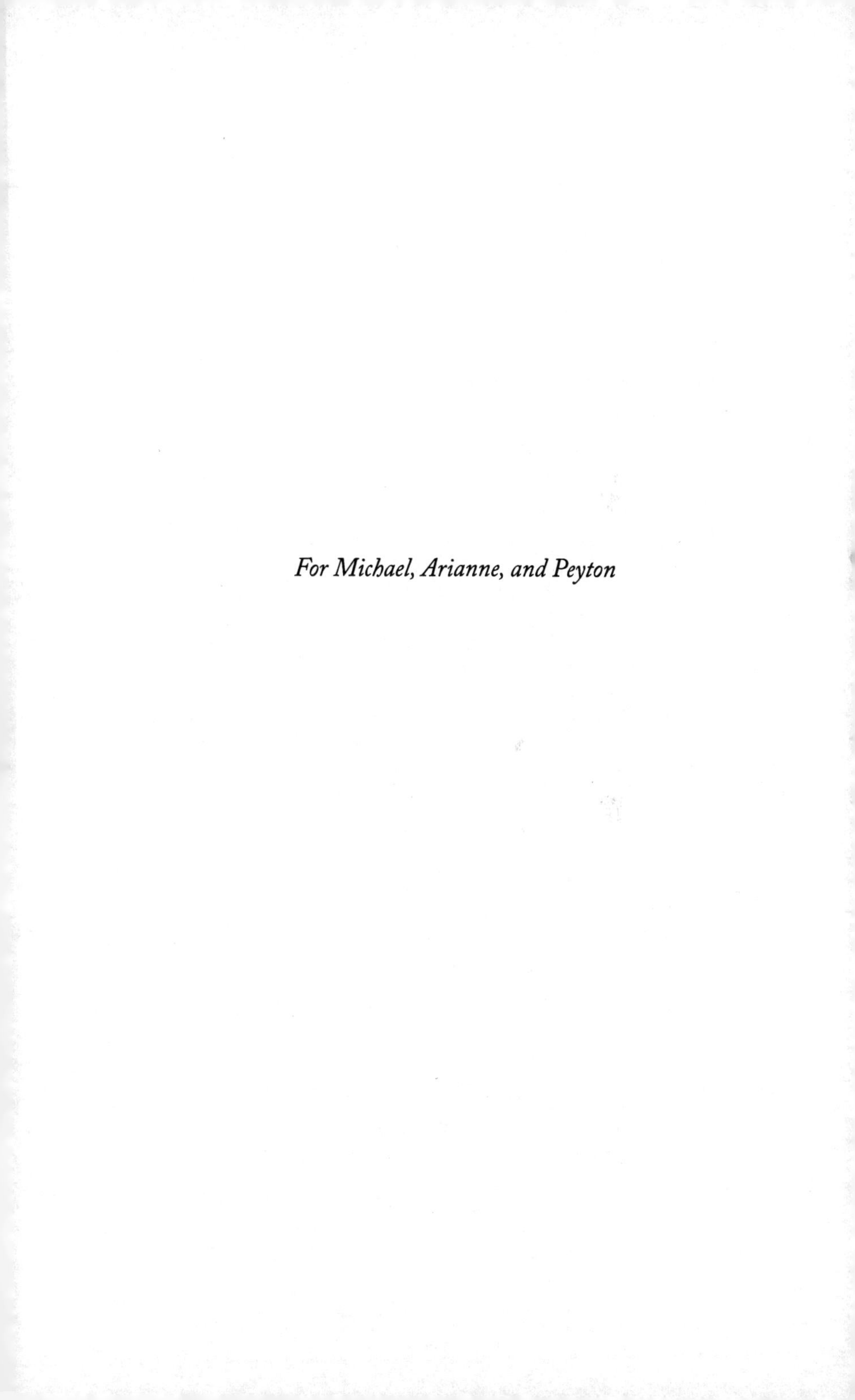

For Michael, Arianne, and Peyton

CONTENTS

ACKNOWLEDGMENTS

Many people helped make this book happen, and I am most appreciative.

I would like to thank everyone at Thomas Dunne Books/St. Martin's Press for being so kind, dedicated, and helpful, especially my editor, Margaret Smith. To paraphrase the great Roger Rosenblatt: a writer produces three paragraphs that he or she thinks sound pretty good until a talented editor sculpts them into one finely crafted, endlessly better paragraph. So, thank you for the brilliant sculpting, Margaret, and for your many excellent editorial suggestions. Thanks also to Lauren Hougen, who missed nothing and moved mountains—and all in record time; to Nadea Mina, who offered excellent guidance and direction; to Joe Goldschein, for all his hard work; and to Dana Skerry, who helped out in a pinch, good humor intact. I would also like to acknowledge Sibylle Kazeroid for her sharp eye and ability to turn a phrase, and Michael Cantwell for his wise counsel.

I am also very grateful to the people at the Carol Mann Agency, including Carol (like they say at the awards shows: "Thanks for taking a chance . . . on an unknown kid!"), Eliza Dreyer, and last—but definitely not least!—Myrsini Stephanides, whose passion, vision, and input were invaluable. I am and will also be forever indebted to Sandi Mendelson for introducing me to a great agent.

To my senior psychoanalyst colleagues at the Institute for Psychoanalytic Education (formerly NYU Institute), Drs. Harold Blum, Theodore Jacobs, and Shelley Orgel, who so generously read portions of the manuscript and provided feedback: thank you for your kindness and assistance. Dr. Blum, your insights on Freud—all offered off the top of your head—were so useful! Dr. Jacobs, your comments about integrating theory were extremely incisive and helpful. Dr. Orgel, you so generously made time to read not just this book, but many of my papers and presentations over the years, and each and every time your edits went where no man (or woman) has gone before. I am forever in your debt. In addition to the aforementioned individuals, I am privileged to have had many wonderful teachers and supervisors during my analytic training and while enrolled in the Clinical Psychology program at Columbia, including Dr. Brenda Berger.

I would also like to express my appreciation to several other learned and giving colleagues, including: Dr. Shelly Itzkowitz, for teaching me most everything I know about interpersonal theory and technique; Dr. Joanne Fishman, for sharing her encyclopedic knowledge of substance abuse disorders; and Dr. Valerie Golden, a true psychoanalytic and Latin scholar, whose continued support and close friendship (and whose unlimited access to PEP abstracts) have meant everything to me.

I am also extremely grateful to Dr. Nancy McWilliams, whose book *Psychoanalytic Diagnosis* had a profound impact on my thinking, my way of understanding character pathology, and my clinical work. And on that subject, I truly appreciate all of the individuals I have treated over the years; I learned from each and every one of you.

To Elena Siebert: I stalked you, but it was worth it! Thank you for your wonderful work, your promptness, and your kindness. And to Rachel Blakeman: recognize the sweater? You should; you designed it!

I would also like to thank family members who have been there for me during this project and beyond: Michael, handsome and brilliant like Don Draper—but the resemblance ends there—your love and support (and reading of numerous drafts) have allowed me to climb mountains and aim higher than I had ever dreamed possible. Arianne and Peyton, awe inspiring and my toughest editors: your insights about what constitutes good writing were spot on—I could never have done this without your cooperation, love, and understanding. Sheila and Joel: you always encouraged me to write, and I am very glad you did. I am also lucky to have many more supportive relatives too numerous to list, including my brother, sisters- and brothers-in-law, in-laws, my many nieces and nephews, and some really great cousins. I expect all of you to buy this book.

Many friends have managed to put up with me over the years, including: Wednesday, a true pal and so helpful in innumerable ways; Erika, Mardee, and Ava, great friends who have always lent support to my writing efforts; and Ari, Alicia, and Elise—none of you watch *Mad Men*, but all of you are now obligated to read every single page of this volume. That goes for you too, Laurie and Karen. Duane: you are off the hook; I know you would have read it anyway, and I thank you for that. Richard: you were right all along; a woman can be ambitious and still be a good mother. I also appreciate all of the friends and neighbors who unfailingly click on my unsolicited blog posts, and who never complain about receiving them.

To Lybi: you know what you did. Thank you. And to Professor Voelker: remember all of your not-so-subtle reminders about active verbs and short sentences . . . and that copy of Strunk and White's *Elements of Style*? Well, they really came in handy.

PREFACE

In a therapy session, circa 2010, a young woman worries about whether she will earn a promotion. "My parents don't understand why I work all the time. They tell me to focus on my social life so I can meet someone, get married. My mother thinks if I don't stop working so much I'll never have a life. I don't agree. I love my job . . . I'm much more a Peggy than a Joan. Peggy knows what she wants—and she doesn't apologize for it."

The colleague who told me about this session knew I was working on a book about *Mad Men*. "I guess you're onto something," he told me. "People are really fascinated by these characters and by that time in history."

Now, I'm no Matthew Weiner, and I don't claim to have an inside track on the show's characters. But as a clinical psychologist/psychoanalyst, I can make some very educated guesses. Writing this book has allowed me to delve into meaty social issues and make polemical claims—practices that my colleagues and I usually consider to be beyond the psychoanalyst's purview.

Most analysts believe that no one can be an expert on another person's psychology. We do not routinely give advice or issue dictates about what a patient is thinking or feeling—nor do we presume to tell patients how to behave or what choices to make. Advice, good as it may be, applies to onetime situations. Advice will get you only so far. Psychic change, on the other hand, goes a long way. It is achieved through the arduous, but very worthwhile, work of gaining insight into personal dilemmas and patterns. Psychic change transcends the onetime situation.

So I do make proclamations, use labels, and even call these characters some rather strong names like "narcissist" (hint: he's tall, dark, and handsome). Why defy psychiatric convention and throw caution to the wind? The characters in *Mad Men* present rich material to be mined. Diagnosing them and examining their inner workings can be an enriching and challenging exercise for those who enjoy dissecting the episodes, clinically trained or not. Plus, my editor made me do it. And once I began, the characters came alive in new and exciting ways. In the end, it was really a lot of fun. (Since you're wondering, the answer is no, I *don't* get out much.) But Don and the gang certainly do. And their exploits are enough to fill a book.

Things sure have changed since Don and Betty set up house in Ossining, New York. On the show, the Drapers have separated and divorced, of course. But in reality and in the larger world, the social, political, and cultural landscapes are now vastly different than they were in the *Mad Men* era. Our society has made great advances: in the workplace, women and people of color now hold many of the same positions as white men. Families look different, as more people choose to be single parents or marry same-sex partners. Society has become less rigid overall. But not all trends have moved in a less restrictive direction. While Don's professional and financial fortunes continued to rise, we now find ours on the decline. We are entrenched in the worst economic crisis since the 1930s. Thomas

Friedman and Michael Mandelbaum, experts on global affairs, have written a new book in which they boldly declare, "That used to be us."[1] They note that a drama is being played out on the global stage, and caution that unless major challenges to our economy, educational system, and government are met, we will continue to lose ground to China and other nations. And so, it is the media that delivers and continues to fuel the message that America has come down. Books, movies, and TV have a profound impact on our thinking. As Andy Warhol once said, "It's the movies that have really been running things in America ever since they were invented. They show you what to do, how to do it, when to do it, how to feel about it, and how to look how you feel about it."[2]

What Warhol meant was that movies not only *reflect* major social trends and changes; they also *shape* cultural norms and expectations. Movie and television stars become the avatars of fashion and style, the messengers of ethics and morality.

And TV's powerful effect continues today. Only now, people emulate the stars of their favorite "real-life" shows. For some, reality TV, with its new breed of celebrity, sets the mark for fashion, design, lifestyle choices, and status, just as the movie stars did in Warhol's day. Fifty years ago the bar was higher, though, and people adhered to a confining, but more mannered, set of social dictates. The Mad Men and women behave in ways that are more formal and less revealing. And they always look great doing it. But underneath their staid dress, pillbox hats, and fedoras lie complicated and puzzling psychologies.

INTRODUCTION

A handsome dark-haired man sits in a crowded, smoky bar writing advertising copy. Oblivious to the noise, mostly male crowd, and glamorous scene, he focuses solely on his work. A uniformed busboy—an older, somewhat reticent African-American man, delivers a drink, and hesitantly answers questions about his favorite brand of cigarette. A bartender—who is white—runs over to the table. "I'm sorry sir. Is Sam here bothering you? He can be a little . . . chatty." "No," the handsome man assures the bartender. "We're actually just having a conversation. Is that OK?" After the bartender exits, the man remarks, "You obviously need to relax after working here all night" (Season 1, Episode 1, "Smoke Gets in Your Eyes").

We find out that this man's name is Don Draper—and instantly we want to know more about him.

Draper is, of course, the central character in *Mad Men,* the series that has spawned a cadre of same-era television and Broadway shows and books and inspired at least one national retailer to offer a line of clothing styled after 1960s fashions. The show's ubiquity and loyal fan base have made it a watercooler mainstay, and have afforded it a certain pop-cultural heft. How do we account for the fact that *Mad Men* has gotten under our skin? It is just a TV show, after all. But its characters are so psychologically compelling, fans of the show watch to see them navigate their difficult and complicated relationships—and to puzzle over what exactly makes them tick. Some may even watch because they identify with Don, Peggy, and the other Mad Men and women, and hold them up as a mirror through which to view and measure themselves.

Plus, the characters are immensely entertaining. Who doesn't get a kick out of seeing Don and Roger knock back a drink—or seven? Who hasn't experienced a vicarious thrill watching dalliance after dalliance, with partner after partner? Watching *Mad Men*, we are like anthropologists studying a lost tribe. They eat that? Their kids run around with dry-cleaning bags over their heads? They smoke cigarettes and drink alcohol at their desks? People *really* used to do those things?

By all accounts, the 1960s were a different time. The characters on the show behave in ways that our millennial sensibility does not sanction or easily comprehend. They get to indulge in ways we cannot. Watching the festival of cigarettes, booze, unprotected sex, cholesterol, and negligent parenting on *Mad Men* entertains, then, because it chronicles what life was like during a more carefree time. Sure, everyone was terrified during the Bay of Pigs crisis. But the show's first few seasons take place before the advent of the late '60s, one of the most explosive times in history. The characters are on the brink of a seismic social shift, but the social and political unrest we know is imminent has not bubbled up quite yet.

We watch as the tension mounts, and we know that major changes in the social, cultural, gender, and political landscapes are about to occur. Even so, life is hedonistic and somewhat safe for Don and company. They know smoking causes cancer, but no one really worries about their health in the same ways we do. No one worries about binge drinking or alcohol abuse. No one wears a seat belt. The kids on the show stare endlessly at whatever is on TV. How different than the current, more restrictive, zeitgeist, which favors healthy behaviors and encourages helicopter parenting. Watching *Mad Men* provides an escape from our more cautious and more anxious modern sensibilities.

Adults need opportunities to escape, to be sure. As Dr. Glen O. Gabbard observes in his book *The Psychology of the Sopranos*, opportunities to fantasize, step out of reality, play, and imagine are important—and not just for kids. Borrowing from D. W. Winnicott, the British analyst who wrote extensively about creativity and child development, Gabbard describes how movies and TV shows (and, it is implied, literature) provide what psychoanalysts call a "transitional space," a vehicle through which adults can engage in much-needed opportunities for play, creativity, imagination, and fantasizing.[1] Play allows adults to enrich their day-to-day experience.

And just how does *Mad Men* allow adults to play? The characters indulge in a worry-free spectacle that provides a source of voyeuristic pleasure for viewers. We vicariously drink, eat, smoke, and engage in affair after affair, things we would not dare to dream of doing. And the escape feels so good. On a more basic level, the show, with its meticulously created settings and costumes, is a sight to behold. It offers all the visual pleasures of a period piece. We are treated to glamour—the dresses are gorgeous, the cars look spacious and inviting (no environmentally friendly compact cars here!), the furnishings and hairstyles take us back to a more formal, even genteel, time. And don't forget those hats! All in all, the show transports us. The corsets, fedoras, furniture, and cars allow us to experience or re-experience a long-departed era, and to get to know a little about the people who lived way back then.

We watch, then, to know the characters in all their complexity, and to see them interact in their relationships. We identify with their struggles with identity, with those about valuing appearances over substance, and with their inner turmoil. We watch, riveted, as they try to find a work-life balance, to get ahead professionally, to stop their self-defeating behaviors and patterns. We step into their shoes and play at solving our personal dilemmas. There seems to be a little bit of Don, Peggy, Betty, Joan, Pete, and Roger in all of us. In them we encounter the mind-sets of our parents or grandparents, and of course, ourselves.

1

Meet the Mad Men and Women of Sterling Cooper Draper Pryce

Things are looking up for the men and women of Sterling Cooper Draper Pryce (SCDP) in 1964. Don has managed to extricate himself from an unhappy marriage and has made a fresh start with Megan, his gorgeous secretary. The admen have freed themselves from the British agency that had taken over their company. And Joan and Peggy have each been promoted. But, as always, appearances do not tell the whole story.

Sure, the office and the people within it look great. The new agency's sleek lines and design are in the style of Mies van der Rohe, and evoke an open atmosphere. But while the ever-so-modern glass partitions may be transparent, the characters within remain closed off, their relationships complex and opaque. Don's true identity; Roger's most recent dalliance with the firm's office manager, Joan, and her resulting pregnancy; as well as Peggy's history with Pete and the birth of their child all remain closely guarded secrets. Don's office romps with Faye, Megan, and others are also kept secret—until he can no longer conceal them.

And while the fledgling firm gives the appearance of prosperity—with 1960s op art and abstract prints adorning the walls, a C. Jeré sculpture in the entranceway, and Danish modern furniture at every turn—what lies within the modern, stylized rooms is pure turmoil: Lucky Strike, which generates the lion's share of revenue for the partnership, has announced that the agency's services will no longer be needed. Glo-Coat Floor Wax defects soon after, despite the shiny Clio Don was awarded for his work on their campaign. After this one-two punch, SCDP's finances become so precarious, it is unclear whether the agency will survive.

With business so tough, the stakes are financially, professionally, and personally high for the agency's employees. They have all bet big on the firm's success—and on one another—leaving the stability of Sterling Cooper for this fledgling agency. Peggy thrives at the office; the workplace provides a major source of gratification for her. Pete bets big on his partner; he loses a $4 million government contract, a huge portion of the business he has brought in, to protect Don from a routine background check (Season 4, Episode 10, "Hands and Knees"). And Don needs SCDP to survive, perhaps more than the others. The agency is his home, professionally and psychologically. At least three of Don's partners (Roger, Bert, and Pete) know that Don has a secret past—and they accept him despite his deception.

Without the agency, Don might have fewer opportunities for employment. He is hiding a fake identity, after all, and not every agency would let that slide. He needs this job; without colleagues like Roger and Peggy to look over his shoulder, and a home to go to at the end of the day, he might fall apart. In psychological terms, Don is someone who desperately needs outside supports like rules, conventions, deadlines, and tough-love confrontations to function. His life becomes especially difficult after his wife, Betty, insists on a divorce and quickly remarries, for example. At his nadir, Don's solace is whiskey, his companions outside the office mostly waitresses and prostitutes, and his life nearly spirals out of control. Just what would happen to Don without a professional setting on which to hang his hat and define his place in the world?

DON DRAPER, MADISON AVENUE'S MARLBORO MAN

Tall, dark, and handsome, stoic and macho—Don is a silver-tongued image-maker who is himself a creation, having stolen the identity of the real Don Draper, a soldier who died serving in Korea. Like the Marlboro Man, the iconic brainchild of admen, the "new" Don exudes confidence, self-assurance, and masculine strength. But for him and the cigarette icon, the machismo is merely a veneer; what lies beneath is darker and more complicated. The actor who played the Marlboro Man is ultimately killed by the very product he hawks, and serves as a cautionary tale and a metaphor for Don's life. Draper and his colleagues suffer under the brutal pace and nature of the advertising game—a ruthless pressure cooker that threatens to destroy those who earn their living making images. Duck and Freddy develop crushing alcoholism. Roger has two heart attacks at the office.

Though Don seems to thrive under work pressures when we first meet him, he begins to fold as his unhappy home environment and secret past close in on him. As his true identity and extramarital affairs become known to his wife, cracks begin to show in Don's refined and competent veneer.

BETTY DRAPER, THE ORIGINAL DESPERATE HOUSEWIFE

A classic beauty from a privileged background, Betty receives a top-of-the-line education and goes on to marry a rising and talented adman, Don Draper, with whom she lives in a picture-perfect house in a wealthy Westchester community. But her glamorous veneer unravels in tandem with her husband's emotional struggles. Soon after Don and Betty set up their beautiful home with their 2.2 children, we see the Drapers begin to grow apart. Don buries himself in his work, seems unable to give much emotionally or communicate with his wife, and has many lovers. Betty fantasizes about cheating with an air-conditioning salesman but remains loyal to Don, though she ultimately does have a one-night stand and an emotional affair with Henry Francis, the man she will marry a short time after the Drapers divorce. Though Betty has all the trappings of wealth and privilege, she has become increasingly desperate and lonely throughout the series thus far.

Being married to a man like Don Draper might explain some of Betty's emotional difficulties, but fans of the show are frequently puzzled by the way in which she grows angrier and angrier, even after her marriage to Don has ended. Some participants in a recent online vote on a popular Web site have even urged Matthew Weiner to kill off her character entirely. Why is she so reviled? Is she merely the angry, rejecting woman fans love to vilify? Like all the others on the show, Betty is more complicated. Her actions are in large part a result of living during an era in which women had few choices, while her psychology reflects her family of origin. We learn, in fact, that what has prevailed is a "like daughter, like mother" scenario; when Betty was a child, her own mother was very much like her, if not worse.

PEGGY OLSON, THE CAREER WOMAN

Peggy, buoyed by her ambition, refuses to be stymied by convention or traditional gender roles. Single-minded in her pursuit of a career, she gets ahead at work and breaks free of traditional male-female boundaries in ways other woman of her time, like Betty and Joan, do not.

Traditional sex roles held that women were subservient and complementary to men—they served as "looking-glasses" for them, as Virginia Woolf famously decried in *A Room of One's Own.*[1] Women were not supposed to compete with or challenge men by taking away jobs and entering the workforce. Sociologist Helena Lopata noted in *Occupation: Housewife* in 1971: "Women [were] expected to move from birth and home-centered childhood into school attendance for a time sufficient to find a husband, but not so long as to waste valuable youth on knowledge used only for a short time. The next appropriate stages [were] work . . . [marriage], giving birth to a limited number of children, rearing children, caring for the retired husband, widowhood, and death."[2]

It was not easy to stray from the social script. Though Peggy refuses to adhere to the rigid constraints of the era, she risks being stigmatized by her refusal to marry or devote her primary energies to the care of men and children.

PETE CAMPBELL, THE BULLDOG

Pete sleeps with Peggy the night before his wedding but marries Trudy, a woman from a social-climbing, wealthy family. Pete's family connections and his wife's father's money allow him to live on Park Avenue, though his salary is just seventy-five dollars per week. And while Pete may have the right address, his ethics are less than sterling—at least at first. In his home life he is selfish and disloyal. He urges his reluctant wife to compromise her ethics and induce a former flame to publish one of Pete's short stories in a national magazine. He cheats on her multiple times.

At work Pete is also cutthroat and devious. He takes a

confidential report out of Don's trash and shares the results with a client in the first of many attempts to go head-to-head with Don at the agency. And though Pete strives to be one of the gang, he does not seem to fit in. He tries to befriend Don, but to no avail. Though his manner is initially off-putting (Don wants to fire him for attempting to break the chain of command but cannot because of Pete's name and connections), Pete ultimately finds a place for himself and learns how to blend in. He and Don forge an alliance that works, as long as Pete does not challenge his authority.

While Pete may be one of the boys when it comes to his devaluing attitudes toward women, he ultimately undergoes a bit of personal development that allows him to break from the group and move ahead of them in his attitudes. We see him become a father and get closer to Trudy. These relationships seem to help mature him and allow him to develop more of an awareness of the needs of others. Likewise, Pete distinguishes himself from the others in terms of his professional standing within the agency.

ROGER STERLING, THE BLUE BLOOD

Roger is cocky, full of bravado, and an elitist. He laughs his way through serious situations, quipping about Miss Blankenship, "She died like she lived, surrounded by the people she answered phones for" (Season 4, Episode 9, "The Beautiful Girls") and announcing, "I've got to go learn a bunch of people's names before I fire them" when the agency is ailing (Season 4, Episode 12, "Blowing Smoke"). He laughs at the world, and eats and drinks whatever he wants, whenever he wants it. But Roger's bravado is a cover-up for his fear—of aging, of his own limitations, and of his frail health.

Like Pete, Roger is well-heeled, the son of prominent family.

But though they are of similar background, they demonstrate differences in their strength of character and levels of resiliency. Roger is fragile and fails to be assertive in the face of adversity, while Pete shows himself to be of much tougher psychological stock—at least for the time being. After Pete fires his biggest client in order to protect Don, he girds his loins and successfully defends himself from Roger's attack at the partners' meeting (Season 4, Episode 10, "Hands and Knees").

Now consider Roger. When he is told by Lee Garner Jr., the heir to Lucky Strike cigarettes, that after a twenty-five year relationship, Sterling Cooper Draper Pryce's services are no longer needed, he makes a sole, emasculated attempt to challenge the decision. Lee tells him that the board's decision is final, and Roger backs off immediately. He conceals this bad news from the partners for weeks, and when they are tipped off by a rival, Roger feigns ignorance. He further deceives them when they insist he call Lee to demand a meeting—which he does, finger pressed down on the dial tone. It is in this moment that we see Roger at his most craven and least resilient. He clearly fears the humiliation further rejection would confer; he does not enjoy feeling powerless and needing anything from anyone else, and he would rather lie to his partners than feel weak or in need with a client (Season 4, Episode 11, "Chinese Wall").

JOAN HOLLOWAY, THE COMPETENT SEXPOT

Joan, the office manager, is a smart and organized woman who is always graceful under pressure—and who is, above all, a survivor. She rises up through the ranks of the secretaries to a supervisory position and is clearly running things at the agency, having earned the respect of the partners for her broad skills. Whenever there is a mess, it is Joan who is called in to clean it up (Season 4, Episode 9, "The Beautiful Girls.")

The capable woman who carries a gold pen around her neck also has a sexual side. Joan struts around the agency in stylish, curve-hugging outfits, and does not mind when all eyes are on her physical assets. She is comfortable with her sex appeal and the power it confers. In the series premiere, Joan unabashedly instructs Peggy: "Go home, take a paper bag, and cut some eye holes out of it. Put it over your head, get undressed and look at yourself in the mirror. Really evaluate where your strengths and weaknesses are" (Season 1, Episode 1, "Smoke Gets in Your Eyes").

Joan's two selves allow her to navigate the difficult and sexist work environment of the early 1960s. In Joan's world, using sexuality is a woman's only way to get ahead. Though she displays an aptitude for the more substantive—and less secretarial—work of reading scripts and finding television advertising opportunities for the agency, she is demoted as soon as a male replacement appears (Season 2, Episode 8, "A Night to Remember"). When Joan is finally promoted, it is only to a glorified administrative position, director of agency operations (Season 4, Episode 13, "Tomorrowland"). Like the professional she is, Joan dusts herself off and heads back to run the secretarial pool each time she is devalued by her male bosses.

CHARACTERS ON THE COUCH

How can we understand these characters, their behaviors, and their psychologies? Psychoanalytic psychology offers the best and most comprehensive approach to understanding human beings and their relationships.

What is psychoanalytic psychology? It is in everyone you see and it is everywhere you look. It is in your spouse's road rage, your coworker's tendency to trip herself up time after time, and a mother's unwitting power struggles with her two-year-old.

When people think about psychology or psychiatry, most think about depression or anxiety, which are common ailments. But in order to truly capture the essence of another human being, it is equally important—and endlessly more fascinating—to consider more than just symptoms and current emotional state. To truly understand another, one must look deeply into his or her psychological makeup; meaning traits or manifestations of personality that stick over time—as opposed to transient moods that can and do change, sometimes quickly and unpredictably. In other words, someone who mopes around and is viewed by family and friends as a "Debbie downer," would be viewed by psychoanalysts as a depressive personality. In addition to noticing that she feels sad, they would recognize her tendency to engage in the lifelong pattern of taking rejection hard, pushing people away, and seeing the glass as "half empty."

If the terms *depression* and *anxiety* refer to someone's current state, those in the field of psychoanalytic psychology concern themselves not just with this, but with understanding that which remains fixed and constant over time: character traits. These are so often responsible for the paradoxes in and the patterns of behavior we notice in our family members, friends, and coworkers.

Who are Don, Pete, Roger, Peggy, Joan, and the rest of the gang at SCDP? They are more than just characters on a popular TV show when viewed through the lens of analytic psychology, the study of people and personality, of personal foibles, patterns of relatedness, and internal dilemmas. Through this lens they become examples of different personality types. They offer an opportunity to expound upon analytic principles and ideas.

Mad Men on the Couch will view Don, Betty, Roger, and the rest of the show's residents through the lens of a psychoanalytic perspective, attempting to shed light on their psyches and explain exactly what makes them tick. The analytic approach provides insight into how our collective thinking has changed from the 1960s to the millennium—and how it has not—and offers a view into the zeitgeist of the *Mad Men* age, the era that shaped who we are today. We can think about how we might confront the challenges faced by the show's characters, and we can wonder: Should we approach things differently today?

In other words, by understanding analytic principles, we can understand not only these characters, but our family members, friends, neighbors, coworkers—and ourselves.

PSYCHOANALYTIC PSYCHOLOGY 101 (FOR THE TRUE PSYCH JUNKIE)

The field of psychoanalysis emerged in the 1880s and '90s in Vienna when Sigmund Freud, Joseph Breuer, and a few other pioneers in this form of treatment discovered that when people said whatever popped into their minds, a process known as free association, they could put into words painful traumas from the past and thus escape being imprisoned by them. Freud famously wrote: "Hysterics suffer mainly from reminiscences"[3] to describe his discovery that with certain patients, once the unconscious was made conscious, their conditions improved. Freud called this "the talking cure."

Freud later modified his theory to explain the different parts of the individual's psyche: the id (instinctual drives), the ego (the rational self), and the superego (the conscience).[4] Once he realized that all parts of the mind had both conscious and unconscious aspects, his original model and technique (uncovering buried layers) no longer sufficed. Freud realized that understanding these different parts of the mind, which are constantly in conflict and cause individuals to repeat the past, was the only way to affect psychological change. His is a one-person model of treatment, in which the patient lays open his or her psychology by talking, and learns through insights to modify aspects of the self that have been impeding progress and causing the individual to get in his or her own way. In this model the analyst is mostly a listener and views himself as an outside observer (as compared to other analytic methods such as the interpersonal one, in which clinicians are seen as active participants, and in which patient and analyst are thought to observe and participate together). This tradition continues today in the school of modern Ego Psychology. Today many orthodox Freudians incorporate theory and technique from other schools; most agree the analyst does not just observe the treatment process.

During and after Freud's lifetime, the field saw the rise of other schools of psychoanalysis, such as the Kleinian, Relational, and Interpersonal schools. Melanie Klein of the British school of object relations believed that personality and pathology formed earlier than Freud had claimed—namely, in the first months of life—and recommended clinical techniques that involved actively confronting early, visceral feelings such as intense aggression, envy, and anxiety. Klein also strongly emphasized the early mother-child relationship as a determinant of personality and psychopathology. She did not believe personality to be solely a function of internal dilemmas (or biological drives), as classical Freudians did.[5]

Where Klein emphasized pointing out primitive emotions, the method of modern Ego Psychology derived from Freud had the analyst inquire about psychological defenses or blocks to understanding, as Freud had written that difficult or unacceptable thoughts and feelings were too painful to know, and were defended against by other parts of the personality. Clinical practice continues in the traditions of Ego Psychology and Klein, as well as other modes that will be elaborated upon. Given the distinction between schools of thought, a present-day Kleinian interpretation might emphasize a patient's wishes to behave aggressively toward the analyst (some call this "speaking to the id"), while a current Freudian might point out that it seems difficult for the patient to know his or her own aggression ("speaking to the ego"). Both schools have in common the belief in an unconscious part of the mind and a view of the individual as being characterized by psychic conflict created by warring internal parts of the personality or by tensions between internal factions and external reality. Insight into one's patterns and internal dilemmas is seen as the route to improved psychological health.

American Relationalists such as Dr. Stephen Mitchell, on the other hand, believed that individual psychology developed within an interpersonal or two-person framework and reflected the early caregiver-child relationship; they deemphasized the role of drives (instincts) in the development and creation of psychopathology, in contrast to the heavy emphasis Freud and Klein had placed on them. (Despite their differing views about instincts, the relationalists did not view the Kleinians as a belonging to separate school, though other groups do draw this distinction). To the relationalists, the psychologies of both patient and analyst played a role in treatment, just as the early parent-child relationship was understood to provide the template for psychological development. For them it was both the insight into the effects of one's personal history on one's present life and the development of a new, "healthier" relationship between analyst and patient (one the patient never had with parents or others), that were seen to be mutative.[6] Despite their differences, the relationalists did have one thing in common with the Freudians and the Kleinians: all stressed the importance of connecting the past to the present during treatment.

By comparison, though the Interpersonal school also began by espousing a one-person model of personality, it has come to reframe classical Freudian theory in such a way that instincts and drives were irrelevant; for these clinicians, as with the Relationalists, it was all about what happened between two people. Interpersonalists stressed the importance of the present and moment-to-moment interactions between patient and analyst to help the patient understand himself or herself; it is such interactions that were seen to afford opportunities for insight and psychological change. One big difference between this school and others: they did not seek to connect past to present as the others do.[7] Confusingly, though, some Interpersonalists do stress the present, and the primacy of "the here and now moment" in their work. Also, such analysts used their feelings as a tool to understand the clinical situation. An interpersonalist might have noticed that a patient was making him angry and ask the patient to clarify what was going on between them, as well as endeavor to understand how and why a patient's anger was affecting the treatment (and the analyst himself). Sometimes interpersonal analysts shared their own reactions with their patients. The issue of whether and how analysts make personal disclosures about their feelings exceeds the scope of this book—suffice it to say it is a complicated matter, and clinicians differ in their comfort level and willingness to share their own emotions and reactions with patients. But the issue of disclosure occurs as often or more with Relationalists, who are more likely to adhere to the two-person (both influencing and observing) model of treatment.

The Freudian Ego Psychologists, Kleinians, Relationalists, and Interpersonalists comprise four major schools of psychoanalysis. Another, the Self-Psychology tradition first developed by Heinz Kohut, believed that Freud's entire model of understanding and treating the individual needed to be revised. Kohut thought that psychological development was arrested when parents were unable to provide infants and toddlers with the necessary repeated intersection of empathy and limit setting, and so a different and palliative experience had to occur in treatment. When the analyst provided reassurances and affirmation previously unknown in order to shore up a patient's childhood psychological hurts, self-esteem was buffered—and over time such empathic interactions helped to satisfy previously unmet needs and to set a path toward a healthier non-arrested developmental phase.[8] The Kohutian approach differs from other methods that involve analysis of different, warring parts of a fully formed self, as had been emphasized by Freud. In order to help, a self-psychologist might focus more on "mirroring," a type of affirmation that is more fully explained in chapter 6, "Family and Child Rearing," and less on confrontation and interpretation leading to insight, all in an effort to give the patient a "corrective emotional experience" (such that by experiencing a new type of closeness or relating, old ills are healed).

Despite the theoretical distinctions I have drawn, most analysts strive to meet the patient emotionally, and will employ any and all techniques or methods of listening that allow true emotional connection to occur. Though we don't all sit in our consulting rooms musing over which is the correct school of thought, a bit of historical perspective about the field is helpful, as Don infamously converses with Betty's Freudian analyst, and Betty meets regularly with Sally's child analyst. Analysis is a part of the fabric of the show—though its presence is not felt as keenly in the lives of the characters as are, say, sex, alcohol, and drugs. But more on that later.

Things in the world of psychoanalysis have changed since Don and Betty's day, and this is discussed in different ways throughout the book. For example, Betty is treated as a second-class citizen; her psychiatrist violates confidentiality and speaks about her sessions and treatment options with Don. Both men view her as a hysterical woman who cannot make decisions for herself, as we will see in chapter 5, "Sexism and Misogyny." Another major change since the Drapers' day: homosexuality was for years considered to be a diagnosable illness, according to the American Psychiatric Association.

The analytic approach still flourishes in many countries throughout the world, though some practitioners have recently turned to cognitive and pharmacological therapies, and Freud's influence remains widespread in our culture. Many people continue to accept his idea that part of the mind is "unconscious," and motivates people in ways they often don't understand, and that they suffer from psychic dilemmas which they address through the use of psychological defenses and compromises. So, when individuals have an impulse, a thought, or a feeling that feels forbidden, they may repress it—only it comes out anyway in a disguised form. For example, when Betty fears loss, loneliness, and the decline of her marriage, she develops disturbances in fine motor control as an expression of her need for attention. Being sick is more psychologically comfortable than needing emotional attention from Don. Despite this "tower of babel," and all of the terms and distinctions I have presented, most modern-day clinicians would not argue that insight into emotions, as well as behavioral and relationship patterns that were set at a young age, helps bring the unconscious into awareness, and aids individuals in improving their day-to-day existence and functioning.

Psychoanalysis and psychoanalytic psychology are not the same, but they remain related fields. While many individuals do not choose to undertake a lengthy and deep psychoanalysis, in which one's earliest experiences and relationships are reawakened and considered in the present day, a process involving many sessions a week over a prolonged period of time, psychoanalytic psychotherapy remains a popular choice for people who want to better understand themselves and break destructive patterns. Analytic therapy might involve weekly or twice-weekly sessions, and is often still based on principles first described by Sigmund Freud.

Despite its detractors, psychoanalysis continues to be embedded in our contemporary culture. And so, the psychologies of the characters on *Mad Men* will be laid out, dissected, and approached from a psychoanalytic perspective. This perspective takes into account the notion that an unconscious part of the mind exists, has an impact on behavior, and plays a role in the formation and lack of freedom from persistent internal conflicts and defenses that keep individuals from making progress in life. It also considers the vital role early relationships play in the creation and maintenance of adult moods, identities, and patterns of behavior.

Which brings us to Don and the gang. These characters exist in a time when great social shifts are occurring—and when seismic changes in our country's cultural and political horizons have come to threaten the status quo. They embody the beginning of a new era, one that pushes our cultural boundaries and results in a shift away from a society bound by a conventional script to one characterized by looser (and loose) mores and norms. It is an era historians and sociologists have called the Culture of Narcissism.

2

The Culture of Narcissism

As mentioned previously, today's world is vastly different than it was when Don and Betty tooled around Ossining in their big, shiny Cadillac. The Drapers would likely not recognize their hometown or Don's Madison Avenue workplace today. Sure, many of the same buildings and landmarks remain. But the people have changed. Attitudes and conventions are radically different. Individual aspirations are bigger, grander. Greed is now acceptable, and is embraced by many. And social scripts have become less conservative. Boundaries and notions of propriety no longer resemble the more formal versions of those existing in the "Camelot" of the '60s. Back then people were satisfied with being middle-class. They valued security, home, and family. A man was considered to be a success if he put on a suit and went to the office each day, and if he could house his wife and children in a comfortable home on a quiet street.[1] Now middle-class is no longer good enough for the many who aspire to affluence; they want luxury items like Sub-Zero refrigerators and Hermès purses—things once sought after or known to only the wealthiest members of society.

This change in individuals' expectations of home and wealth has been on the horizon since Don and Betty's day. Like the Drapers, most boomers could expect income levels to rise and opportunities to present themselves in virtual perpetuity. Life was so good for this cohort, in fact, that their expectations began to differ from those of prior generations, and they began to exhibit the first signs of the sort of entitlement that runs rampant today. According to Dr. David J. Rossman, a psychiatrist interviewed by Studs Terkel in *Hard Times*, an oral history of the Great Depression: "Now people think it's coming to them. The whole ethos has changed."[2]

The characters of Don, Betty, Roger, Joan, and others reflect this shifting ethos, and their individual psychologies reflect the changes in the human psychic structure that would come to characterize the modern era. In the words of Dr. Nathan Ackerman, another psychiatrist interviewed by Terkel, before Don's time, "People who came for treatment were preoccupied with internal suffering . . . [Now], they don't contain the disturbance within their own skin . . . get into difficulty with other people . . . [Before Don] people felt burdened by an excess of conscience . . . an excess of guilt and wrongdoing . . . [Since the late 1960s] there's no such guilt."[3]

What these post-Depression era psychiatrists meant was that many people in Don's day and beyond began to have consciences that were different than those of their grandparents. Whereas most who lived in the years after the Great Depression saw their problems as self-created, and lived according to rigid internal standards, many who live now are more likely to attribute their troubles to external causes, to possess a sense of self that is less intact, and a conscience that is less self-blaming. What would be most apparent to observers and innocent bystanders who interact with such individuals, though, is that these people suffer from internal fragility and stagger around with bruised egos. To put it simply, they are narcissists.

Those afflicted with narcissism cannot bear to feel painful feelings such as self-doubt, anxiety, shame, and inadequacy, so instead they twist feelings and perceptions until they experience the threat as outside of them. When someone twists reality as a matter of course, and as part of day-to-day existence, it distorts that person's internal experience and weakens his or her sense of self, altering the conscience. Thus, narcissists become less self-recriminating and assume less personal responsibility for their problems.

Individuals who blame others are able to transfer their own intense emotions to an outside scapegoat, ridding themselves of their overwhelming maelstrom of feelings. Since narcissists believe that what feels bad was caused by someone else, they feel and act entitled. As the interviews in Terkel's oral history of the Great Depression reveal, people of prior generations felt more responsibility for their own lives and problems. There was a greater propensity to look inward and a greater desire for self-understanding, both of which were seen as a means to address individual pain and suffering.

As mentioned, the process of looking inward was to become less popular during Don and Betty's time. According to Christopher Lasch, historian, social critic, and author of the 1978 classic *The Culture of Narcissism*, self-understanding was no longer valued by Americans, individually, or as a culture.[4] His remarks are in line with prominent psychoanalyst Otto Kernberg's formulations of narcissism; those who feel deprived and broken find such feelings intolerable, and act quickly to rid themselves of their pain. Today, as was the case in Don's era, action and blaming continue to be on the rise; quick fixes are sought. Many now prefer a pill to take away the pain, or a Botox injection to excise an unwanted facial line, thus eschewing the sort of deeper introspection that requires both ownership of psychic pain and a commitment of time to address the underlying disturbance. Roger's reacting to his fear of aging with a hasty marriage to the much younger and very beautiful Jane is a perfect example of dealing with a psychological affliction by seeking an external quick fix, instead of attempting to address emotions head-on.

Another prominent analyst, Heinz Kohut, views narcissism as a self-esteem problem; a condition characterized by an individual's sense that he or she possesses a fragmented and faulty self. Feeling broken and inferior, and terrified of falling apart emotionally, afflicted individuals spend all of their time—and focus all of their efforts on—attempting desperately to repair this perceived damage and bolster self-esteem.[5] This is one reason such people appear so internally preoccupied and selfish.

Kernberg and Kohut provide explanations for the prevalence of narcissism on an individual level. Lasch and Terkel also place it in a social context. Reading them leads one to conclude that the rise in modern levels of narcissism is also a function of the decline of social groups and hierarchies. Don and Betty's era saw a proliferation in the divorce rate and the breakdown of a rigid social script. Before their time, individuals adhered to norms and respected institutions such as marriage, family, religion, and community. They joined and took active part in them, and were thus exposed to rules and constraints. Being part of a society, family, and community meant limits, doctrine, judgments. Disturbing problems, overwhelming feelings, and outsized grandiosity were contained by the presence of groups and hierarchies, and their confining ideas about acceptable behaviors, attitudes, and mores.

As noted, in the early 1960s the vast majority of individuals respected authority, believed in institutions, and routinely adhered to social norms. Most had faith in our government and in its paternalistic abilities.[6] So, when did all of these changes in the politics, government, and international landscapes begin to occur? Up until the mid-1960s, in fact, the Boomers were booming. Americans felt hopeful and expected expansion; the nation's fortunes were on an upswing. We won wars. We made it to outer space—*Sputnik* was launched by the Russians, but John Glenn and Neil Armstrong were ultimately the first to circle and walk on the moon.

The events of November 1963 changed everything. President Kennedy, young and handsome, with his glamorous wife and cute kids projecting an image of vitality, was publicly and brutally shot. His assassination—and Abraham Zapruder's footage, which was shown widely on TV—robbed Americans of their innocence. Until that afternoon on the grassy knoll, Americans believed their fortunes would always rise; they viewed the country as an immortal superpower.

Christopher Lasch wrote *The Culture of Narcissism* not long after the occurrence of many events depicted in *Mad Men.* His ideas about cultural narcissism were so revolutionary that President Jimmy Carter invited him to present them at the White House. The president noted that Lasch had identified a major cultural trend and described a seismic shift that had occurred in America: a society comprised of self-absorbed, shallow narcissists had collectively come to embrace the superficial. Lasch argued that given these shifts, Freud's definition of narcissism needed to be revised.

When Freud treated patients at the turn of the last century, censorship was rampant. During these years, individuals could not openly discuss sex, or emotions that differed from the proper, staid post-Victorian sensibility. As a result of social constraints, many ideas and feelings were forbidden, and thus psychologically repressed. Individuals developed somatic (physical) reactions such as paralysis and fainting; and some even became intensely phobic or depressed, much like the fictional heroines who died of broken hearts and could never leave their dwellings. These were the patients that Freud had treated.

Lasch's contemporaries were markedly different than the individuals whom Freud had seen and written about almost a century earlier. Since that time, the types of character and symptoms exhibited by individuals afflicted with narcissism had changed drastically. Drawing from Otto F. Kernberg, a psychoanalyst who is perhaps best known for his writings on narcissism, Lasch defined contemporary narcissists as individuals who feel empty, are desperate for attention and admiration, tend to have unsatisfied oral cravings, engage in shallow relationships, and use others to gratify their desires. In addition, he described how those so afflicted attempt to rid themselves of intense feelings of rage and self-loathing by acting out aggressively toward family members, coworkers, and friends, a far cry from the repressive behavior exhibited by prior generations.

Lasch believed that a backlash against overly permissive 1930s and '40s parenting styles had caused the narcissistic personality to become prevalent in society. According to him, "debased versions" of Freudian theory (including notions like "children must be allowed to express all feelings or they will develop a complex") had robbed parents of their authority (and had robbed children of soothing and limit-setting adults who make the world a predictable and safe place). He claimed that it had become fashionable for parents to turn to expert dictates about what constituted good child rearing, instead of following their instincts and responding to what babies and children needed. The doctrine of the times told them when and how to feed, bathe, nourish, educate, and socialize their children. Raising kids was no longer the purview of parents; it had become a social construction.[7]

This shift away from individual parenting and toward experts, rules, and doctrine had interfered with good mothering and healthy patterns of attachment, according to Lasch. He concluded that changes in parenting style were responsible for the prevailing and widespread occurrence of narcissism in many individuals.

NARCISSISM: THE DIAGNOSIS OF THE MILLENNIUM

The term narcissistic personality disorder refers to one of the personality disorders described in *The Diagnostic and Statistical Manual of Mental Disorders* (DSM).[8] Narcissistic personality disorder persists throughout life and is characterized by difficulties in relationships, intense emotionality, and problems in overall functioning (those prone to it suffer from frequent depression and feelings of emptiness, for example). Criteria include lack of empathy; excessive entitlement; a grandiose sense of self-importance; feelings of emptiness, envy, and intense rage; a preoccupation with fantasies of success, greatness, power, and brilliance; a need for admiration; a belief one is special; a feeling that one can only be understood by a few special individuals; and the tendency to interpersonally exploit others. Narcissistic personality disorder describes an individual's seemingly arrogant attempts to compensate for a brittle self, one characterized by persistent low self-esteem and feelings of emptiness. *The Culture of Narcissism* describes a culture-wide and societal shift first identified by Lasch: Americans have collectively become a nation of shallow, self-absorbed narcissists.

While Lasch was not writing about the fictional adman Don Draper, he would easily recognize Don's struggles with self-esteem and his difficulties in relationships. Though he is successful at work and has a beautiful home and family (at least initially), underneath it all, Don suffers. His self-esteem depends on the maintenance of a successful image. He cannot tolerate limits, mistreats women in relationships, and acts in entitled ways. He is grandiose in his attitudes toward clients and coworkers. He walks out of meetings, thinks his pitch is always the best and most important, and at times displays an inflated sense of his worth—even though he is a talented creative director. If a client disagrees with him or says no to him, he feels injured and becomes angry.

THE NEW FACE OF NARCISSUS

In Greek mythology, Narcissus was a beautiful young man who gazed endlessly at himself in a reflecting pool. He was so overcome by his reflection—and so in love with his image—he could not avert his gaze from his own likeness. Narcissus perished because of his self-involved state and his inability to look away from his beautiful reflection.[9]

While Don doesn't stare at himself in a reflecting pool, he runs from one attempt at salving his injuries to another. Like Narcissus, he is preoccupied with his own thoughts, needs, and desires. But Don's psychology and narcissism go deeper than his self-serving outer layer seems to suggest.

As we have seen, Don possesses many of the qualities discussed by Lasch. He behaves aggressively, especially toward his wife and brother, but also toward his lovers and clients, and acts as though he is above the rules, not subject to marriage vows or army discharge regulations. He is also psychologically fragile, leaving him easily insulted and prone to take things personally. And when Don gets angry, watch out (recall his fury at Pete's disloyalty, and his rage at what he saw as Betty's flirtation with his boss). If he is confronted with a problem he doesn't want to address, he runs.

Let's take a closer look at Don Draper, the polished 1960s adman constructed by Dick Whitman: his psychology, his psychological diagnosis, and his complex relationships with others.

In Season 1, Don's much younger, idealizing half brother, Adam, shows up unannounced at the agency and unwittingly threatens to blow Don's cover. Don arranges a meeting just to tell Adam he cannot have any relationship with him. He coldly leaves five thousand dollars in cash in a suitcase and attempts to push all thoughts of Adam out of his mind—until he learns that Adam has hung himself (Season 1, Episode 11, "Indian Summer"). What motivates

Don to turn his back on his gentle, trusting half brother, and what do their interactions reveal? Don single-mindedly protects his false identity despite considerable personal cost. His insistence on maintaining his image ultimately pushes his brother over the edge and contributes to Betty's decision to end their marriage.

Don's creation of a new identity is one of the major themes of the show, and for good reason. The issue of how identities and personalities form and shift provides one of the greatest puzzles for both philosophers and psychoanalysts. Philosophers have long wondered what the essence of mind is; what is real and what is perception? Descartes thought that thinking proved that a mind existed.[10] Plato argued that all that could really be known to an individual, given the filtering effect of the mind on the outside world, was something akin to a shadow on the wall of a cave.[11] Kant proposed a distinction between what is real (noumena) and what is perceived (phenomena). He argued that we could only know that which was perceived, and not that which truly existed in the natural world.[12]

Then came Freud. He set out to explain perception and the mind in a different way. He wrestled with the issue of reality and instinct as well as with how the mind was constructed and how character and identity were formed. In his classic paper *Mourning and Melancholia*,[13] he set out to write about the difference between mourning and depression, but his insights also shed light on one of the ways personality takes shape; namely, through processes of incorporation and identification, which involve the infant and toddler taking in the words and interactions he or she has had with his or her parents. This develops over the course of millions of moments over several years. Today a child's personality and conscience would be seen by Freud and others as continuing to develop after toddlerhood, until the child reaches the age of five or six.[14]

According to Freud's writings on depression, the processes involved in grieving explain how people take on aspects of others. This is similar to what happens as personality is forming, and is a normal part of development. There are two ways this happens: either the child becomes exactly like his parents without discrimination (a process called incorporation), or he adopts only certain aspects and attributes of their personalities while discarding the rest. Incorporation works like this: say a toddler tells her doll exactly what her mommy has just told her, using exactly the same words and mimicking her mom's tone and posture verbatim. Children routinely and normally do this as they develop and mature. They ape parents, teachers, and other role models, seeming to swallow them whole in their mimicry. Don's serial cheating can be understood as the incorporation of the prostitute mother he never knew, as well as of his philandering father. Sexual promiscuity is a core part of his identity. This total and indiscriminate taking in of the only thing he knew about his mother shaped how his character formed.

Another building block of personality, "identification," is a process that involves a more subtle, less dramatic "ingesting" of the other. Instead of just becoming a mini-me like the toddler who mimics her mother, or Don, who becomes like his mother, a child who has identified with someone else might choose (though not necessarily consciously) discrete aspects of a parent's personality or character and discard others. So, Don's becoming a workaholic, like the father who spent day and night tending to the farm, is an example of his taking on an aspect of the elder Whitman, as part of his personality. By comparison, Don's promise to his son, Bobby, that he'll never lie to him (he wants so badly to be emotionally present for his children) taken together with his disappearance from his daughter's birthday party (in effect he abandons her, just as he was abandoned) is an example of identifying with a hated aspect of a parent, despite all best efforts not to do so.

Suffice it to say, personality development and identity formation is a complex and multidetermined process for Don—and the rest of us. It is both conscious ("I want to be tall like Daddy") and unconscious (if parents yell and scream all the time when resolving disputes, children will imitate this behavior when attempting to work things out with siblings and peers, for example).

The term *identification* will come up again later when I explain why Peggy is so mean to one of the other secretaries. Don't be confused! Identification has two meanings; it occurs as part of healthy development but can also be the result of a defensive process, employed by individuals attempting to deal with their own aggression and survive difficult situations.

No discussion of identity would be complete without a few words on development of self-esteem. Though this is complicated, and is also addressed in chapter 6, "Family and Child Rearing," and in the discussion of mirroring that follows on page 46, the formation of identity and self-esteem has much to do with how children are treated by adult family members. An individual who is constantly told she is stupid will come to believe this over time. Likewise, a girl who is told only that she is pretty and who is treated as an ornament (or a house cat!) will think of herself as a second-class citizen and might not feel competent or worthy. Take, for instance, Betty, who needs a man to take care of her, and Joan, who accepts second-class treatment at work and in her personal life.

Back to Don. We already know his entire persona to be a creation. At the most basic level, he has crafted a new identity in order to escape reality both immediate and psychic. Hiding his desertion from the army ensures his physical safety and survival while also allowing him to escape the emotional and mental constraints of being Dick Whitman. "Don" embraces his new persona wholeheartedly, finding a beautiful wife, and establishing the perfect home and family in a comfortable suburb. On the outside,

Don and his wife, Betty, project an image of success, wealth, and sophistication. They seem to embody the American Dream. Maintaining this image is of the utmost importance to Don. He seems to think that if you look good, you feel good; if you appear to be successful, you are successful; if you pretend something bad never happened, it didn't.

When Don's brother, Adam, surfaces, his presence threatens the maintenance of Don's shaky house of cards and the new reality he has so carefully crafted. Don has to repudiate all knowledge of Adam in order to preserve his identity. His intense self-preoccupation makes it difficult for him to empathize with Adam's feelings. For him, image trumps relationships.

As we will see over and over again, Don's image is his lifeline. Psychologically, it provides a means to achieve emotional well-being and survival. Sure, he looks arrogant. He appears to be full of himself every time he stomps out of meetings or hits on a beautiful woman, but such actions are merely compensatory, and represent a cover-up of feelings of inadequacy. The smooth veneer he has created represents an effort to remake a self that feels damaged and broken into one that others view as sturdy and impressive.

Don constantly needs bolstering, and often maneuvers to prop himself up. In order to do this he sometimes denies the more vulnerable aspects of his internal reality that are too unsettling to bear. When Don takes out an inflammatory ad in the *New York Times* to decry cigarettes and smoking, for example, he is attempting to compensate for a pair of recent punches to the gut: Lucky Strike's departure and his partner Roger's inability to hold on to the firm's largest client, both of which threaten the future of the agency (Season 4, Episode 12, "Blowing Smoke"). His grab for attention, admiration, and influence seems to be just a big power play and an attempt to spin a positive image, but it is also a desperate attempt to compensate for a fragile internal state.

What has caused the weaknesses in Don's character and the damage to his self-esteem? Don had scant opportunities to identify with loving parents. His mother was dead and his father worked all the time and seems to have been emotionally absent. His interactions were mostly confined to the slights and sneers of a critical and rejecting stepmother. Her jibes and criticism made it hard for him to develop solid self-esteem. There was no one to soothe him or help him deal with his own feelings of loneliness, sadness, and anxiety. A maelstrom of difficult feelings constantly swirls around inside of him, testing his coping mechanisms and strength, leaving his ego bruised and in a weakened state.

Despite his emotional problems, Don likely won't seek therapy any time soon; he routinely expresses negative opinions about psychology, psychiatry, and psychoanalysis. He is not a big fan of these disciplines—or of mental health treatment.

We learn his attitudes toward the field in the pilot episode when a research psychologist is retained by Sterling Cooper to help prepare an ad campaign for Lucky Strike, a client in the tobacco industry. The psychologist—Dr. Greta Guttman, complete with Viennese accent and stern demeanor—attempts to tell Don that smoking is a manifestation of Freud's ideas about the death wish.

"Freud, you say? What agency is he with?" quips Don.

Don summarily dismisses the psychologist's ideas and her field, stating, "Psychology might be great at cocktail parties, but it so happens that people were buying cigarettes long before Freud was born." He calls her "Miss" instead of "Doctor," and ultimately throws her report in the garbage (Season 1, Episode 1, "Smoke Gets in Your Eyes"). Likewise, Don practically hangs up on Betty's doctor when he recommends multiple sessions a week for psychoanalysis (Season 1, Episode, 11, "Indian Summer"). His distaste and mistrust stem from his history of early loss. Like many fragile people, Don instinctively avoids exposing feelings, the true nature of which he might not be aware of. Sometimes he is able to rid himself of the tumultuous emotions; other times he cannot, and his unconscious mind haunts him, making him feel out of control, broken, and defective.

CONTROL FREAK?

We see over and over again that what Don cannot control makes him feel desperate and anxious. The deaths of his parents and lack of parental love have left him full of longing, anxiety, rage, depression, emptiness, and desperation. These emotions are persistent and overwhelming, and Don must constantly control or get rid of these emotions and his longings to keep himself from falling apart.

Like all human beings, Don uses psychological defenses or maneuvers, often unconsciously, to change or control the direction his mind takes. One of Don's mainstays is denial, automatically pushing feelings and parts of himself down deep to create a new identity, as discussed. Another of his defenses is isolation, as in Season 4 when he compartmentalizes his feelings about the past and present, seemingly thinking, "The agency's crumbling; I'll marry Megan to get through my utter desperation and persistent anxiety." His conscious experience is simply falling in love with her. He is so unaware of his motivations that he tells her, "I don't know what it is about you." She reveals what it is when, in answer to his statement that she knows nothing about him, she says, "I know who you are now" (Season 4, Episode 13, "Tomorrowland"). What a powerful aphrodisiac for Don! The past is out of mind, his present anxiety and desperation are split off, locked away as if in a separate compartment, and his sole focus is on the immediate future. In addition to isolating unpleasant thoughts and feelings, Don also tries to pr himself from unwanted emotions by using "splitting," an uncon scious defense through which he seeks to rid himself of overwhelming anger, anxiety, desperation, and depression. Don, in the blink of an eye, unconsciously twists reality at every turn—and with each twist, he perceives the threatening feelings inside of him as coming from an outside source. So, it is the *other* who is angry and has wronged him, or the environment that poses a threat. Splitting is a vestige of the normal infant/toddler tendency to view someone as "all good or all bad." Through soothing and predictable interactions with parents, children come to see individuals as possessing aspects of both good and bad. Don, though, sees others in black and white, "all or nothing" terms.

Don's use of splitting causes major distortions in his experience and perceptions, and difficulties in his relationships—in a nanosecond a person who was loved and idealized automatically becomes all bad, even hated. For example, when Faye encourages Don to look at his past, the idea of embarking on a process of self-discovery, and of stirring up depressing and dangerous emotions, terrifies him. Faye and her psychological approach are instantly all bad; Don is finished with her. He immediately moves on to the young, glamorous, and maternal Megan (Season 4, Episode 13, "Tomorrowland"). Similarly, when Betty questions Don's hiding of his identity, financial information, and numerous infidelities, he is finally forced to reveal his true identity. After being rejected by Betty, Don learns from Roger that Betty has feelings for Henry. Don forces her to admit this, then quickly turns the tables to rid himself of painful feelings of loss. He becomes victim instead of participant in the failure of their relationship: Betty is the cause of the problems in the marriage; *she* needs a doctor because she is not well. With this "split," Betty instantly goes from wife to enemy—he calls her a whore, threatens to cut off economic support, and turns completely cold, though ultimately he does not challenge her decision to seek a divorce (Season 3, Episode 12, "Shut the Door, Have a Seat").

Fans will recall that Don later tells Anna Draper about his separation, "I had it coming," which is seemingly contradictory to the view that Betty is all bad. While it is true that Don has moments of insight, they are fleeting. Though he may have a moment of clarity, he does not really ever connect the knowledge and consequences of his actions to his own emotionally driven behaviors—and so any self-awareness is transient. Don's use of splitting represents an attempt to exert control over his mind, and over all situations, feelings, and people that make him anxious or threaten his perception of himself. Sadly, it has the opposite effect, weakening his sense of self. Thoughts and feelings that are instantly cast off become confusing, leading him to wonder, "Did I really think or feel that; if not, how do I really feel?" And topics or emotions that are pushed out of consciousness, like Don's fear of losing those he loves, feel unspeakable, shameful, and become even more threatening to him.

Don's splitting is not apparent to the naked eye. To bystanders he merely appears to be inflexible, a dictator who forces others to do things his way. He walks out of client meetings with Menken's department store and Jantzen swimwear when they don't like his pitches. Likewise, when Roger confronts Don after Jane falls into his lap—she is drunk—Don tells Roger he's making a fool of himself. Thereafter, Don avoids his senior colleague, and harbors a grudge.

While Don might be called a "control freak" by some, his attempts to spin his image, leave his past behind, and force others to comply are compensatory, even desperate, measures taken to prevent perceived losses of self-esteem and thwart crippling feelings from puncturing his already wounded self.

The tendency of Don and others like him to isolate and split off feelings raises an important question that is a theme of the show: Can people ever change? In Don's case, the sad answer is probably not. His chances of significant emotional and psychological change do not look good because he acts on impulse to get himself out of sticky situations. He does not make the connection that his behaviors have brought about adverse consequences in his life. He does not learn that they have a negative impact on him or others. Rather, he just acts, seeking to excise any unwanted thought, feeling, or circumstance. He desperately moves to immediately change that which he does not like. When he does have a transient insight into the role he plays in creating his own problems and difficulties (like his moment with Anna), it is gone as quickly as it has appeared. We can expect him to repeat exactly the same patterns going forward.

Though Don is on an upswing at the end of Season 4, having grabbed onto Megan to bolster his fragile self-esteem, his suffering is hardly behind him. When his psychological maneuvers have failed to temporarily relieve him of his despair in the past, Don characteristically acts out, using woman and booze to cover up and ward off that which frightens and depresses him. Though things are bright with Megan—for now—Don will be up to his old tricks as soon as there's a new bump on Madison Avenue.

Don's little girl, Sally, has perhaps the best chance of making meaningful emotional and psychic change. Engaged in a treatment with a child analyst, she is the only one on the show who is actively examining her feelings and relationships with others. Though Sally is struggling with difficult feelings, and though she acts out by cutting her hair and masturbating in a neighbor's home, she is engaged in a process of trying to understand the meanings of such behaviors. When she takes the train into the city alone to see Don, it follows her analyst's suggestion that she walk home from camp, and represents a step toward achieving her own autonomy. One measure of a successful child treatment is that it has allowed the child to progress from one phase of development to the next. Since the treatment began, Sally has gone from a lisping, confused girl to a tween who is figuring out herself, her body, and her relationships with others. She, more than any other character on the show, is making meaningful internal changes. Like Peggy, Sally represents the next generation, which has a new, and better, way of doing things.

Don Draper's senior partner, Roger Sterling, also struggles with bruised self-esteem and with difficulties managing emotions. Like Don, Roger acts instead of understanding internal dilemmas that arise within him. His wealthy background and his father's position as one of the founders of an early incarnation of the agency would seem to have insulated Roger from difficulties typically faced by adults, such as financial or workplace problems. But money and social position cannot shield him from his emotional problems. Raised by nannies, Roger seems to have lacked love or warmth as a child, and he cannot sustain meaningful relationships. He casts off his first wife, is not close to his daughter, and uses Joan whenever he feels like it. Feelings terrify Roger, so he minimizes and denies them. Having experienced the deprivation and trauma of fighting in a world war, he tries to cover up any emotional or physical frailty by joking about his situation—no matter how high the stakes.

ROGER'S NARCISSISM

Roger's wealth and station in life have left him lacking in resilience and prone to humiliation. Born to privilege and earning for years the generous sums paid to an advertising executive, he hardly lives off of his salary. Bert chides Roger about losing the Lucky Strike account, "Lee Garner Jr. never took you seriously because you never took yourself seriously" (Season 4, Episode 12, "Blowing Smoke"). As if to prove Bert's point, Roger backs down when things get tough at work. Roger feels he does not need to fight. He would rather preserve the patina of a prideful, blue-chip image than do something he considers beneath him or even humiliating, like flying in to appeal to Lee's board.

Roger is unable to grovel to clients because it would bruise his ego too much. He is prone to feeling sorry for himself. He is also arrogant, having been raised in a privileged family, and considers hustling for work to be beneath him. After he cheats on his first wife, Mona, with a teenaged model at the agency, he appeals to Mona in a childlike voice when she rushes to his side after this dalliance causes him to suffer a heart attack (Season 1, Episode 10, "Long Weekend"). Likewise, Roger begs Joan to come to his side because he needs her when Lucky Strike leaves. When she criticizes him for keeping the precarious position of the firm a secret and not giving the partners an opportunity to save the account, he says: "You know what it's been like walking around with this for weeks? I have a hole in my gut" (Season 4, Episode 11, "Chinese Wall"). Roger often plays the victim, using women—especially Joan—to coddle him, and as such, fails to take responsibility as an adult for his behavior. When he encounters adversity, such as a mugging or the loss of his biggest client, he turns to Joan for comfort and reinforcement.

Why isn't Roger more resilient? Jean Macfarlane, author of a seminal study on those who came of age during the Great Depression and in the years after, speculates that hard times made many children of the depression era strong, for "no one becomes mature without living through the pains and confusions of maturing experiences."[15] Growing up privileged, without hardship and deprivation, there were no challenges to strengthen Roger's ego, and he never built up the more resilient aspects of his character. Roger never had to work terribly hard, thanks to his family's money and social connections. He is given to feelings of entitlement, and habitually approaches life by putting pleasure above most else, eating ice cream sundaes at his desk and always ordering rich foods. And of course, Rogers drinks and has sex whenever the mood strikes. He hasn't had to work in the nuts and bolts of the business and relies on his creative team to come up with the concepts—he just has to wine and dine the clients.

Roger's insouciant attitude toward life and his self-indulgent behaviors are the result of growing up affluent and pampered. But even as it has its rewards, wealth and privilege have scarred Roger. Economists have written about the tendency of individuals to value things based on scarcity. At least one economist, Staffan Linder, has noted that those raised with or who acquire privilege and material wealth and the trappings and possessions it yields tend to value each acquisition less than those who do not acquire wealth and material goods.[16]

Roger's love of earthly pleasures is not merely entitlement, though. His self-serving behaviors represent attempts to salve old wounds, and to compensate for underlying insecurities. Roger's war injuries were not physical, but psychological. Like many in his generation he did not have a choice and was sent far away from his family to serve. There was nothing familiar, no comforts, and no security. It was a terrifying existence. He lived and fought under harsh and brutal conditions with no protection from the elements—or from enemy warfare. His daily existence involved the trauma of watching as friends and compatriots were maimed and killed right before his eyes. So, Roger's idyllic country-club existence was immediately shattered when he began his tour of service. He saw firsthand, and at a young age, exactly how tenuous human life can be, leaving him with a persistent fear of dying and losing his health.

Such feelings did not go away after the war had ended. Seeing so many young people suffer and die filled veterans like Roger with sadness, and these losses constituted a heavy and painful burden, day after day—as did the survival guilt of living through the war when so many others had not. Roger's intelligence would surely have led him to wonder, "Why not me?" The senselessness and injustice of random deaths would plague him and others in his generation until old age. Men like Roger believed that they weren't men unless they were tough, though. They did not discuss feelings, and most of them viewed seeking emotional support as a sign of weakness.

Back to Roger's entitlement. Unable to acknowledge his fear of death and survival guilt—what kind of man would that make him?—Roger pushes his psychic life underground. He tries to bat the bad memories and sad, terrified feelings away; they are a threat to his masculinity and stability. We know this strategy does not work; he cannot forget his war years, and repeatedly uses military lingo and combat metaphors, just as he remains rabidly angry at the Japanese. So he makes other attempts to compensate for his destabilizing emotions. One compensatory measure is seeking almost constant pleasure. It is as if Roger thinks: "I can do whatever I want and act in any way I want because I have earned it after what I have done for my country and what I have been through." He even tells Don that his generation drinks because they "deserve it."

FOREVER YOUNG

Roger's entitled attitude toward life is also apparent in his relationships with women. He cheats on his first wife, the long-suffering Mona, with many younger women, and has a meaningful and prolonged affair with Joan. Mona truly adores Roger and stands by him during two heart attacks. Yet he casts her aside and decides to marry the much younger Jane, who makes him feel good about himself. Jane has almost no life experience—she stumbles around tipsy at their Derby party and falls all over Don. Similarly, she has no idea how to endear herself to Roger's daughter, Margaret, who is her age, and she flounces around like a spoiled child when Roger tells her that her behavior is inappropriate (Season 3, Episode 3, "My Old Kentucky Home").

Marrying Jane is a shortcut, and this is Roger's modus operandi: he is used to things going his way without his having to work too hard to bring about that which he desires. When he marries Jane because he admires her youth and beauty, his desire for her reflects his wish to enhance these qualities in himself. In Greek mythology, Zeus devours his pregnant consort, Metis, and by swallowing her whole, he incorporates into himself Metis' virtues of cunning and diplomacy and gains advantage in battle.[17] Much like Zeus, Roger swallows Jane whole when he marries her for the qualities she possesses. He imagines that if he aligns with the youthful, vital Jane, he too will become younger and forestall the aging process. But Roger's marriage to Jane is ill-conceived, as Jane is not a mutually mature partner. His shortcut did not work and we see him at the end of Season 4 looking dissatisfied as his young wife hugs him.

Roger uses women for his own designs and returns to his comfortable, married life when he is through with them. What appears to be selfishness and a tendency to use Joan for his own designs is actually a deeper problem. His fear of aging, common to those who are vulnerable and insecure, explains his serial philandering and juvenile behavior. "If I have sex with all of these beautiful young women, maybe I will be forever young," is what he seems to think. And he acts on his fear time and again.

While married to Jane he reinitiates contact with Joan, and once again finds himself in the position of being married to one woman while in love with another. Joan is an important figure in Roger's life. He turns to her after his heart attack, when he is seeking solace and support. He seeks Joan out again after he loses his biggest client. In each instance he reveals his fear of being weak and old, for instance immediately surrendering to a mugger, with no effort to fight back or defend Joan (Season 4, Episode 9, "The Beautiful Girls"). Their relationship is intimate and their connection solid—perhaps because Joan sees Roger clearly and accepts him for his weaknesses: the pampered, self-involved, and fearful aspects of his character. Despite Joan's generosity, Roger uses her selfishly for his own designs and casts her aside time and again on a whim. Joan is always there for the taking. She acts like a mother who allows a toddler to explore the world but is still always there for him emotionally. She accepts the child's need to roam and supports this by being present at his will, a secure base that is available whenever he wants to return. She protectively and maternally applies makeup to his face so he can go into a meeting with important clients after a massive heart attack.

During Roger's scenes with Joan we wonder whether his is as transient a feeling as it has been in the past. Joan must also feel this way. She has a pregnancy and a husband at basic training to deal with; nevertheless, she soothes Roger in a light and upbeat manner. She pats, placates, and tends to him as if he is a sullen toddler. Joan combines beauty and sexuality with maternal protectiveness, and Roger is perpetually drawn to these qualities.

Roger is not alone in his narcissim. Pete can also be narcissistic in his dealings with others. The night before his wedding he shows up on the doorstep of Peggy, a virtual stranger, and they have a tryst, which he then tries to pretend never happened. He does the same with a neighbor's young German nanny. When Pete uses and discards women, we see him at his most unempathetic and narcissistic. At these times, Pete cannot see past his own immediate wants and needs.

And like the men of SCDP, Betty is clearly narcissistically vulnerable. She behaves in cold and unempathetic ways with her children and fails to see them as separate individuals, worrying only how they reflect on her. Like Don, Betty engages in splitting, most notably in the Season 4 finale, "Tomorrowland," when she fires Carla. The loyal babysitter immediately becomes "all bad" in Betty's eyes after she allows young Glen Bishop to see Sally, as the boy stirs up complicated feelings of jealousy and serves as a reminder of an unhappy time.

Like the others, Betty is full of disturbing emotions that leave her psychic self ready to cave at any given moment. For her, image and reputation are valued over self-awareness. In Season 4, she dresses Sally and Bobby up in beautiful clothes for dinner with the Francis family on Thanksgiving. But her need to put forward the picture of the perfect family is so great it limits her ability to parent. Sally does not like the food that is served, but Betty's emphasis on appearance over all else limits her ability to see her daughter's needs. She forces Sally to eat what she does not like, causing Sally to vomit on the fine china and shattering the perfect family image. By forcing Sally to eat against her will, Betty sends the message that she has usurped control over her daughter's body. Such intrusiveness could over time set Sally up for later problems, like the development of an eating disorder.

Don, Betty, Pete, and Roger can be said to exemplify the walking psychologically wounded. They did not receive the emotional goods and mirroring necessary to build solid self-esteem.

WHAT LASCH FORESAW: NARCISSISM NOW

Lasch's arguments about the overall character and symptoms of narcissism (which are transitory and exist to some degree in everyone, not just those afflicted with narcissistic personality disorder) continue to be relevant today on the individual and cultural levels.

People who feel empty, full of self-loathing and desperation, who act in entitled and grandiose ways, and who cannot sustain meaningful relationships are everywhere. Such traits are exacerbated by the ubiquity of the camera and the value we place on fame—the narcissistic personality has actually become fashionable, and narcissists are viewed as successful. And because the narcissist craves attention, and in frequent cases, fame, many who suffer from this problem are willing to reveal increasingly private aspects of their lives on reality TV shows or through social media channels. It is not uncommon for some to discuss their sexual exploits via Twitter, to text (or "sext") compromising photos, or to post all-too-revealing images online. There are no longer boundaries of any sort in America. And with this rise in levels of narcissism and the resulting decline of boundaries, the focus on family and community has changed. The zeitgeist has shifted; instead of valuing home, family, and security, as individuals did in the era of the Great Depression, individuals have come to prize fame, attention, money, and fortune above all—even personal relationships.

Lasch blamed the prevalence of narcissism on the millions of anxious parents who had stopped listening to their instincts and were not tuned in to their children because their reliance on expert doctrine did not allow for relationships based on instinct, empathy, and attunement, and, in his view, rendered parents unable to provide emotional support to their children.[18] Betty does even less than the parents Lasch described; whenever her children need something from her, she is not emotionally available; she often retreats or becomes angry. While Lasch condemned those who abdicated all parental responsibility to experts and books, we can only wonder what he would make of Betty. She would never expend her energy on learning how to parent, and she says as much.

Betty's missteps, explained more fully in chapter 6, "Family and Child Rearing," can be used to illustrate what type of parenting children really need in order for healthy development (the measure of self-interest and-esteem we all need to live and thrive) to occur. According to Heinz Kohut, whose theories of self-psychology, explained in the section titled "Psychoanalytic Psychology 101," contributed to our understanding of narcissism and development, individuals need to have parents provide responsive, loving attention in order to prevent developmental arrests and injuries to self-esteem.[19] Parents who go by the book are unable to provide the mirroring their children so desperately need.

The concept of mirroring is complicated, but it essentially boils down to this: in order to develop self-esteem, individuals must see themselves affirmed time and again in the eyes of a loving parent. So the baby who says "goo goo goo" needs a responsive parental "goo, goo, goo"—and responses such as this over the course of the baby's first years demonstrate that what he or she is thinking and feeling are validated by his or her mother, and allow the baby to learn over millions of esteeming moments that what he or she thinks and feels is acceptable and worthy. This allows the baby to feel buffered and loved. Infants and children need to see a gleam in their parents' eyes in order to feel loved, respected, and admired, which is necessary for healthy development. With failures in mirroring come bruised self-esteem—and this plagues the individual for the rest of his or her life.

Failures in attunement explain a lot about the prevalence of narcissism in the modern day. But unprecedented levels of aggression due to society's breakdown in limits, rules, and doctrine have also contributed to the rise of grandiosity and overblown expectations. When an infant's aggression is not regularly neutralized over repeated and routine interactions with an empathetic and tuned-in caregiver who provides soothing (and so helps the infant to feel less overwhelmed by this emotion), it becomes all-encompassing and threatens to devour the mind. It becomes so overwhelming, in fact, that when such an infant becomes an adult, aggression can become a problem and feel dangerous. In other words, when angry, individuals prone to difficulties with aggression might feel paranoid, might worry about going crazy, or might imagine the mind spinning out of control. Such rage and associated fears of losing control become intolerable and must be immediately split off or acted upon because they are so frightening and terrifying.[20]

If you are wondering why everyone on the show seems to exhibit narcissistic pathology, you are not alone. Narcissism has become so prevalent in our society, some in mental health disciplines have even called for its exclusion from the next edition of the field's diagnostic manual—if everybody has it, what is the point of diagnosing or classifying it? While this might seem counterintuitive, it demonstrates just how ubiquitous narcissism has become—not just on our favorite fictional TV show, but in real life.

The working relationships of Don, Roger, Pete, Peggy, Joan, and others at the agency offer a window into how they exhibit narcissistic personality traits, as well as how they bump up against one another—both at the office and after hours.

3

Working Stiffs

Rich, white Anglo-Saxon Protestant men dominate Madison Avenue in the 1960s. The women at Sterling Cooper are all secretaries and office managers—until Peggy comes along. Sexism, and even harassment, is the norm at the office; no one even blinks when women are routinely objectified. Even lewd images of Joan, posted by the creative team, go unremarked upon until Peggy confronts the perpetrators (Season 4, Episode 8, "The Summer Man"). Sexual romps and drinking are considered part of a day's work, part of blowing off the stress of the job.

And Don, Roger, Pete, and the rest of the staff work nonstop. In their hierarchy, the men are always at the helm, and the women are in positions of service. Feminist author Germaine Greer discussed workplace sexism in her book *The Female Eunuch*, and relayed popular directives for secretaries that had been published in the *Sunday Times* of London, including: "Always use deodorant . . . learn how to make good coffee and tea . . . and always look beautiful." According to Greer, "A secretary was expected to become a graceful and necessary piece of office furniture" and like his wife, was a status symbol for the boss."[1]

And as writers like Greer tell us, things were not easy for women in the workplace back then. Those who wanted to do more than administrative work struggled to forge their own paths. There were no role models to copy or examples to follow. Things continued in this way until a few female pioneers broke ground. But their impact was not widespread and was limited to individual workplaces. It was not until television gave us examples of working women that more people began to accept their existence.

Before Peggy Olson, millions embraced Mary Tyler Moore's character of Mary Richards, the quintessential single working girl whose pluck and typing skills landed her a job in a newsroom and whose ability to navigate tough personalities and tackle workplace issues allowed her to nail it. Richards proved she could successfully walk the line between assertive and aggressive; she was never strident, and always looked great in her funky 1970s getups. She was attractive without being sexually provocative. When she eventually worked her way up to producer, she proved a woman could "make it after all," even if she was a single girl in the hard-core manly world of television news.

Many Americans' opinions about working women were based on what they saw Mary Richards say and do. Before her, female sitcom characters were mostly starched, smiling housewives in pearls, whose role in the family—and main goal in life—was putting the roast on the table and urging well-mannered children to do their homework. These TV stay-at-home moms lived life in the service of others, like Betty Draper was expected to do.

Mary blazed the TV trail, and society based its opinions about working women on her. Without Mary we might not have had the Peggy Olsons of the world—on television or in real life.

PEGGY WORKS HER WAY UP

Peggy, the sole female copywriter at Sterling Cooper, starts as an entry-level secretary and works her way up to become a highly valued member of the creative team. At first the men do not take her or her ideas seriously. But given the chance to write a few lines of copy, she impresses them all with a revolutionary concept for Belle Jolie lipstick: "Mark your man." She shines again when she is pulled in to test and write copy for an exercise machine: "The Rejuvenator—you'll love the way it makes you feel" (Season 1 Episode 11, "Indian Summer").

Ultimately, it is Peggy who distinguishes herself over everyone else—male and female—when the agency's biggest accounts defect and she and Ken Cosgrove bring in Topaz Hosiery. She tells Joan, "I just saved this company!" (Season 4, Episode 13, "Tomorrowland"), and proves herself to be a rainmaker—she can bring in clients despite her gender.

Psychologically, Peggy is driven and sole-minded in her pursuit of success, but she is not so wrapped up in herself as to be unable to recognize the needs of another human being. Though her comment about her new hosiery client's "saving the company" sounds grandiose, Peggy is not a narcissist in the clinical sense. She does not exhibit the kinds of disturbances to self-esteem, self-regulation, and relationships that others (most prominently Don) do. She retains her healthy self-esteem and follows her own instincts, even when her family questions her choices (Season 4, Episode 7, "The Suitcase") and her male coworkers talk down to her. She shows herself to be able to have successful and mutual relationships as well. Peggy can be a friend to Don, Duck, and Freddy. She seems truly concerned about their struggles with alcohol, and it is she who comforts Don when he is in need. And she tries to protect her female coworkers from sexism and mistreatment. These interactions show that Peggy, unlike Don and Betty, does not lack empathy for others.

As the show demonstrates in Peggy's awkward interactions with other women, she would not have had much in common with many women in her cohort, like the 571 Chicago-area women who participated in sociologist Helena Lopata's 1960s study of women's roles. Many said that their primary role was to marry and be a housewife and mother. They almost unanimously said that being the best wife to their husbands was the "most important thing"—not surprisingly, a career was considered the least important of all possible social roles by a majority of these women.[2]

The rare woman who did not share these traditional, domestic goals was often viewed with suspicion and skepticism. To paraphrase Germaine Greer, career was almost a dirty word; most women would not want to admit they engaged in a masculine activity that required them to suppress their feminine being and exploit personal relationships, as those in a career must do.[3]

At first Peggy tries to be exactly like the other secretaries, flirting with Don and applying lipstick in the bathroom. But he quickly puts a stop to it when she coyly strokes his hand. Shortly thereafter, when she distinguishes herself in a focus group and is given the opportunity to write copy, Peggy embraces work. She shuns everything and everyone, putting her job first. She tells Pete, "I could have shamed you into being with me . . . You got me pregnant. I had a baby. And I gave it away . . . I wanted other things" (Season 2, Episode 13, "Meditations in an Emergency"). But, like the famous ad says, "Is she or isn't she?" Pete and Peggy are constantly at odds, but he looks longingly in her direction on more than one occasion. Trudy, nine months pregnant, spots Peggy in the bathroom and attempts to provide the consoling and soothing remarks she thinks a single woman wants and needs to hear: "You know, twenty-six is still very young." Peggy does not share Trudy's worry about a woman's decision to focus on a career. She has chosen her professional life over her personal life—at least for the time being.

As a newly appointed junior copywriter in the early 1960s, Peggy doesn't feel she has any wiggle room or any rope for mistakes and missteps. She unwittingly finds herself between the proverbial rock (stereotypes that have bound women) and hard place (the baby that is growing inside of her). Her dilemma is profound; it is one path or the other. She has already begun to rebel against her Catholic upbringing by going on the pill, sleeping with Pete, and showing ambition. She has worked hard and has taken steps to forge her own path, at Sterling Cooper and in the rest of her life.

Despite her apparent successes and outward strength, Peggy is not without psychological struggles. It takes a strange form of courage—and some complex psychological maneuvers—to fail to notice a baby growing inside of oneself. Peggy's religious upbringing and single woman status contribute to her denial, a psychological defense that occurs automatically and unconsciously, like a knee-jerk reflex to a doctor's tap with a mallet. Peggy really does not know she is pregnant all those months. She simply cannot see what is too painful—and her mind brings this about in order to protect her from the painful awareness that she had done something her family, her priest, and even she herself disapprove of; she has conceived a child out of wedlock—and she will have to give that child up to achieve her new dream. Additionally, her denial saves her from having to make a painful choice: save herself and her career and the new identity she has been fighting so hard to forge, or choose her unborn child and the domestic path of motherhood, a road she is not yet ready to take.

Peggy chooses work, as always. But the moment the baby arrives, Peggy's denial is punctured. She crashes and winds up in a hospital bed, suffering from an emotional breakdown (most likely postpartum depression). People who experience a profound loss commonly grieve in stages. At first they fail to apprehend the situation, then they react with anger and perhaps attempt to change it, and ultimately they arrive at some form of acceptance. But Peggy's depression and denial are prolonged. Ultimately it is Don who helps her. Don's advice seems to bolster her. "Do whatever they say. Peggy, listen to me. Get out of here and move forward. This never happened. It will shock you how much it never happened" (Season 2, Episode 5, "The New Girl"). Soon after she is back at work, having put the pregnancy and the baby behind her. All that remains of this period in her life is the secret emotional connection she and Pete continue to harbor.

We will see Peggy struggle with impulses toward activism. She questions SCDP's choice to represent a client that does not hire any people of color, but does not make waves when she is told that is not her agency's concern. Similarly, she befriends Joyce Ramsay, a lesbian who refuses to be bound by traditional female dictates of subservience to men. Such events seem like they may foreshadow Peggy's increasing activism in future seasons of the show.

DON AND PEGGY'S SECRETS

When Peggy breaks the mold it frees up those in her orbit to change their behaviors as well. Take Don. In interacting with Peggy, he breaks out of the constraints of his 1960s WASP culture and his provincial upbringing. Don respects Peggy, and many times shows her more kindness and empathy than he does Betty. Why is this? Peggy has talent, ambition, and puts work first. She earns his respect. She tells him, "I know what I'm supposed to want, but it just never feels right, or as important as anything in that office" (Season 4, Episode 7, "The Suitcase"). In her Don has found a kindred spirit. Her ability to break through traditional gender constraints is a reward she earns through hard work and ability. It allows her boss to interact with her in new and different ways.

By contrast, the Drapers' interactions fit a template, and their behavior is subject to rules and societal dictates—all of the niceties required of those in their social group. Betty can only be Don's wife and the mother to his children. She was brought up to be the beautiful wife of an upper-middle-class WASP businessman. She did not challenge this destiny, and society gave her no other blueprint for married life. So, there were no opportunities for her to depart from a conventional script or for the Drapers to stray from suburban 1960s norms. She is not supposed to wear a bikini, converse with men unless her husband is present, or go into the "big city" to model. She is not expected to think and have ideas that stimulate discussion with her husband. She is more of an ornament than a peer. Don's expectations of Betty, which are in line with her own views about herself, combine with rigid social dictates to keep Betty in the grip of a limited existence. She can only be wife and mother—but more on this later.

Not so with Peggy. Once Peggy begins to show her competence and drive (characteristics then viewed as masculine), she is not just a maverick, but an unknown. Don is not forced into a stale and limited way of relating to her. In their interactions, the slate is almost blank; there are few expectations in how he views and classifies her. And once he begins to view and treat her like someone with abilities, interests, and a mind of her own, she becomes more of a peer, and their friendship grows. And the seeds of this friendship are sown when Don visits her in the hospital. He takes her under his wing, saying, "Do whatever they say [to get released]. . . . This never happened." Don gives his very best advice, advocating forgetting and compartmentalizing, the strategies he uses to get through life's toughest moments. His interest and advice reveal how much Don cares about Peggy. He chooses to protect and mentor her in a way he does not do with anyone else in his life. It seems to do the trick. Peggy is soon back at work and does indeed manage to put the pregnancy behind her.

Fast-forward: Don struggles to survive under the weight of a divorce and limited access to his children, as well as the double blows of the imminent death of his friend Anna and financial problems at the agency (Season 4, Episode 7, "The Suitcase"). He appears to be falling apart: drinking to the point of forgetting directives to his staff, blacking out, and even vomiting and fistfighting at the office. Don's mainstay (denying feelings) no longer works when life is closing in.

Don seems to be alone in the world—until Peggy steps in and offers her friendship. Over the course of a long evening together, Don reveals a lot about his history: he watched his father die, he grew up on a farm, and he served in Korea. He falls asleep with his head on Peggy's lap, and she is there with him the next morning when he calls Anna's niece and finally learns the news of Anna's death. Don allows Peggy to see him in a vulnerable place; drunken and damaged with vomit on his shirt and tears in his eyes. He tells Peggy that "the only person who ever really knew me [has died]." "That's not true," counters Peggy (Season 4, Episode 7, "The Suitcase").

Don's exchanges with Peggy reveal Don at his interpersonal best. Only Peggy seems to see all aspects of Don, and it is only to her that he reveals a full range of feelings, such as anger, sadness, and fear—all of which haunt his daily existence. Don's life, as we already know, is organized around running from feelings and from the truth. He disguises his identity and crafts a new persona, he drinks to forget, and he displays bravado and acts fearless whenever he is frightened. But with Peggy, Don is authentic. He argues with her (instead of walking away, as he does with so many others). He cries in her lap. He is emotionally intimate with her. After Anna, she is his one true friend.

TRANSFERENCE AND OEDIPUS REX

Don mentors Peggy and nourishes her ambition, but he has zero tolerance for Pete's arrogance and the abrasive tactics he uses to get ahead. But Pete is from a well-to-do family, and Don cannot fire him. The firm needs his name and the doors it opens for them. Don isn't crazy about Pete to begin with; Don had to work his way up in the world and do everything on his own—he views Pete as a spoiled brat and does not respect his reliance on family connections and fancy schools to advance himself. Plus, Don's low self-esteem and tendency to take things personally cause him to hold grudges and lash out at those whom he perceives to have wronged him. And Pete continually challenges Don's authority and tries to upstage him, causing additional tension between the men. On one occasion Pete even pitches Bethlehem Steel executives a campaign idea behind Don's back during a private dinner, infuriating Don, who views this as overreaching. Clearly, both men want to be in charge, but only Don can do the creative pitches that please the clients. Pete brings in work, but Don is the image-maker.

One explanation for Pete's tendency to butt heads with Don: Pete unconsciously relates to him like a significant figure from his past. This type of interpersonal engagement is known as transference, and is a phenomenon that is ubiquitous, according to psychoanalysts. It involves a psychological process in which old feelings, ideas, and ways of behaving and relating toward a significant person from childhood are transferred onto a person in the present. Pete acts unconsciously toward Don in ways that recreate Pete's relationship with his father. We know Pete's father is rejecting, belittling his job in advertising and berating him for doing nothing with the family name (Season 1, Episode 4, "New Amsterdam"). Pete challenges Don and wants to replace him, yet he also idealizes him. Pete goes straight to Don when he learns the elder Mr. Campbell has died—he seeks mentoring from him, and guidance about how to handle difficult situations and how to behave at work and in the world. When Roger invites him to join the new agency—they need his "talents"—Pete looks at Don and insists, "I want to hear it from him" (Season 3, Episode 13, "Shut The Door, Have a Seat"). And Pete remarks at another point, "It matters to me that you're impressed" (Season 1, Episode 13, "The Wheel"). Pete resents Don, yet he knows how much he needs him to spin the pitches and the campaigns. He routinely bumps up against Don's seniority and power.

In other words, Pete has "daddy issues," as they have commonly come to be called. The concept of the Oedipus complex is based on the Sophocles tragedy *Oedipus Rex* and on the Greek myth that Freud drew from in order to elaborate on a boy's or man's primal drive to kill or replace his father and sleep with his mother. Some analysts believe that girls possess a similar Oedipus-type fantasy called the Electra complex. Skeptics can consider the episode in which Sally runs away and lands at Don's office. She tells him, "I love you. I want to live with you all the time. I'll be good" (Season 4, Episode 9, "The Beautiful Girls"). She even tries to cook for him. Her comments and behavior are consistent with the unconscious desire, common to young girls, to replace mommy and marry daddy. In the play and the myth, Oedipus unknowingly kills his father and marries his mother. When he eventually learns what has happened, he gouges out his own eyes.[4] Unlike the tragic king, Pete doesn't kill anyone in the literal sense, but he certainly tests Don and challenges his authority, and possibly dreams of surpassing and replacing him, even as he respects and needs him. Likewise, freelancer Joey Baird is disrespectful to Joan because she reminds him of his mother, who was also an office manager. Both men's transference complicates their work relationships and causes tension at the agency.

Don also has a strong transference of his own: he views Conrad Hilton as a father figure. They meet at Roger's country club and bond over their outsider status. While Hilton is wealthy and can afford private clubs, he is all about work; country clubs and the superficial pursuits of the rich leisure class hold no appeal for him. He and Don have that in common. And while Hilton takes an interest in Don, he makes Draper prove himself. A good pitch is not enough to win the account or Hilton's confidence. He puts Don through the paces, making him redo a campaign (even though his request for an ad for hotels on the moon is unreasonable—and even he knows it). He acts like a father who is making his son earn his place in the world. And the two men develop a close father-son tie until a British rival threatens to take over Sterling Cooper, leading Hilton to terminate his business relationship with Don for good.

So Don's heated feelings and the nature of his father transference cause him to argue with Hilton in the workplace. Similarly, Pete's feelings about his father and their relationship cause him to argue with Don. Peggy and Don argue too, but their struggles are due less to her feelings about her family of origin than to sociological factors, as she is fighting a restrictive social code. While Pete tries at times to upstage Don with Bethlehem Steel, Peggy is loyal to him; she heeds his instructions and embraces the guidance he offers her. She butts heads with him and challenges him, but she does not covet his job. She isn't trying to take his place at the table—at least not yet. She's just happy to be invited to the party.

Now on to Pete's attitude toward work, which overall can be said to differ from those of his colleagues. Pete may have "daddy issues," but he does ultimately partner with Don, Roger, and Bert (and eventually the Brit Lane Pryce). Unlike the other three Americans, however, he did not fight in a war or experience life during the Great Depression. The chronology of his birth places Pete in a different generation than that of these partners, and is significant in terms of his psychology.

Pete's attitude toward adversity has much to do with the circumstances of his life and the timing of his birth. He shows himself to be resilient by weathering a few hard knocks from his father-in-law and at the office. On the home front, Trudy's father will only mete out a tiny tranche of his large business to Pete. He may seem spoiled and entitled for asking, but he shows himself able to weather rejection. Though the small portion of business his father-in-law offers embarrasses and angers him, he weathers the snub, takes care of the business, and goes after numerous other larger clients. While at work he withstands obstacles and adversity—even the loss of a huge $4 million account that Don makes him jettison, unbeknownst to the other partners—and remains professional and stoic even when Roger lambastes him for what appears to be ineptitude (ruining the client relationship and bungling the opportunity). In these ways Pete never seems to give up, proving himself to be more resilient than some of his colleagues.

Glen Elder Jr., the sociologist who studied children of the Great Depression and the impact of that era's deprivation and hardship on them and the generation that followed, noted the difference between children of the Depression and their children, who like Pete, were college students in the 1950s and early 1960s, and were inclined to take for granted a reasonable or comfortable standard of living. Earnings and prestige were not the important considerations in choice of a job for many of Pete's generation. Their outstanding priority centered on the job's growth potential and its contribution to others and their personal suitability for the work."[5] Pete, like Roger, was born to wealth and privilege, had access to higher education, and has been able to choose a profession not for security, but for "intrinsic" factors, such as the opportunities for creativity it affords.[6]

But though Pete grew up wealthy, his father squandered the family fortune, as did many wealthy families of the Gilded Age. Pete becomes a working stiff who is expected to earn a salary. Pete uses his father-in-law's business and his own boarding school connections to bring in new business, even manipulating and strong-arming his father-in-law to hand over an account so Pete can support the baby he and Trudy are expecting. Over time, he shows himself able to function as a partner. Eventually he is the leading generator of revenue for the agency, and he begins to self-righteously resent his partners. When the firm is contacted by the American Cancer Society, he notes with sarcasm, "Great, public service, free work. That's just what we should be doing right now." At another point he comments, "Am I the only one who brings in any business at this agency?" (Season 4, Episode 12, "Blowing Smoke").

Like other privileged men of his time, Pete has a superior attitude, and uses others for his own designs. While Pete matures over the course of the show, he is the least psychological of all the characters—he doesn't look inward often and his focus is mostly on the present and on his comfort. Pete's trajectory from spoiled frat boy to competent adman and father supports the contention of sociologist Jean Macfarlane, director of the Berkeley Guidance study of outcomes of the Great Depression, that being exposed to some hardship and deprivation shapes character and builds resilience.[7]

JOAN vs. PEGGY

Joan has learned through experience and hard knocks that she can wield only one type of influence: the power of her sexuality that is achieved by being close to the white men of the ruling class. She is allowed to do so only indirectly, though. She is not permitted by the men of Sterling Cooper Draper Pryce or society to allow the competent self to prevail, separate and apart from the sexual one. Though Joan hits what we now know to be the glass ceiling, Peggy manages to break through. Interestingly, Peggy's ascent in the agency causes tension with Joan that culminates in the scene where Peggy uses her power and position as a copywriter to fire a male colleague who objectified Joan and mocked her with a salacious drawing. Joan not only refuses to thank Peggy, but instead berates her in a brutal fashion: "I'd already handled it . . . So all you've done is prove to them that I'm a meaningless secretary and you're another humorless bitch" (Season 4, Episode 8, "The Summer Man"). Peggy represents a new kind of woman, one more like Faye, who can get ahead based on her smarts and hard work yet still be feminine and attractive. Joan never breaks out of the older mold of sexy secretary who ties her fortunes to a successful man.

Perhaps due to their different career trajectories, there is always tension between Joan and Peggy, although they share a laugh and confirm their commitment to the agency when Don impulsively marries his much younger secretary (Season 4, Episode 13, "Tomorrowland"). Joan is clearly stymied. She marries a doctor, but cannot get any farther than office-manager-without-a-raise on her own merit. While Joan derives power from being close to powerful men, such as Roger, Don, and even Lane, she does not claim power on her own by using her intellect and asserting herself in that way, as Peggy does. In fact, she rails against Peggy for humiliating women by handling sexism in a direct way and playing right into the classic male stereotype of the overbearing masculine woman (Season 4, Episode 8, "The Summer Man"). In Joan's view, this makes things worse for all women at the agency. When she is treated like an inferior woman, her approach is to handle things on her own, quietly and with humor. She prefers not to make waves to get what she wants, and not to confront men's power directly. She views Peggy's behavior as masculine, and her words as strident. Joan prefers to take a softer, more "feminine" stance.

Joan certainly begrudges Peggy her promotion. When she leads the new junior copywriter to an office with a door, she remarks, "I said congratulations, right?" Peggy nods. "Once people get what they want they usually realize their goals weren't that high" (Season 1, Episode 13, "The Wheel").

Even as Joan congratulates Peggy, her tone is contemptuous. Her intention to deflate Peggy at her moment of success is clear.

The women butt heads because their approach to the workplace is so different. Peggy is defining a new brand of woman, and Joan resents her for this. Peggy is more like Faye. Both rise to professional positions and are treated in relatively less sexist ways by professional male peers, though Peggy does have to endure sexist comments even when she is running the show (in one meeting, Stan, the new art director, implores Peggy to take off her top, then takes off his pants) (Season 4, Episode 6, "Waldorf Stories").

Peggy is viewed as humorless and aggressive when she fires a male coworker who devalues Joan, but she has adopted the male qualities of Don (assertiveness, using power to manage people) and the female qualities of Faye, and in so doing has developed a new model of office behavior. Faye is seen as a professional and treated in kind. And Peggy seems to imitate her manner and clothing style. Both women do their jobs by day and have some kind of social life after hours. They are not at work to get married, but they look womanly, feminine, and attractive to their colleagues.

Perhaps most important, Joan resents Peggy because she believes the younger woman has usurped her power. Joan was the boss. She taught Peggy the ins-and-outs of how to survive at the agency. She issued warnings and dictates and enforced workplace rules. When Peggy began to write copy, Joan made it clear that she was still required to complete her secretarial duties—anything extra came out of her own time. When Peggy turns the tables and breaks out of the secretarial pool, it rankles Joan. The younger woman has managed to do what Joan could not and never will. They are sometimes allies, but Joan's competitive and envious feelings complicate their relationship and their ability to forge a friendship.

THEY DON'T MAKE 'EM LIKE THAT ANYMORE

Miss Ida Blankenship, the hard-of-hearing matronly office veteran, is another one of SCDP's working stiffs. Joan assigns Miss Blankenship to answer Don's phones after his callous wooing and casting off of the secretary du jour has caused a tearful resignation and exit. Miss Blankenship barrels in, and what she lacks in adeptness, polish, and finesse, she makes up for in willingness to serve the firm. We learn that her current appearance does not tell her entire story—she was sexy and promiscuous in her day, as Don and Peggy discover when they drunkenly play the tape of dictation Roger has made for his secret autobiography (Season 4, Episode 7, "The Suitcase").

Don and Peggy's glance into the past reveals that Ida Blankenship has been with SCDP and its previous incarnations for years; she does not run away from the pressures of Madison Avenue or from the abuses commonly endured by the secretaries of her era. When she dies—at her desk, of course—the mood in the office is awkward and uncomfortable. Everyone searches for the right thing to say. Bert insists she be brought to a funeral home, not the county morgue. Roger quips (in trademark fashion), "She died like she lived, surrounded by the people she answered phones for" (Season 4, Episode 9, "The Beautiful Girls").

Roger's insensitivity aside, Ida Blankenship is revealed to be a true staple of the office—as much a part of the culture of SCDP, as even Bert, Roger, Joan, and Don.

While Miss Blankenship's bumbling phone manner provided comic relief, her death shed light on the relationship between Don and Joan. When questioned about why he puts up with Miss B.'s loud, indiscreet phone manner, Don defends her—and Joan's staffing decisions. He tells Peggy that the older woman was exactly what he needed.

Clearly, Don and his partners defer to Joan's judgment in administrative matters. And it is Joan who is called in to deal with the mess that is the newly dead, slumped-over elderly secretary—front and center in the office. Joan coolly and efficiently pulls a blanket over her, allowing a client meeting to proceed without further incident.

Ms. Blankenship is somewhat cartoonish, and clearly serves as a comic foil in Season 4. Although her story is not fully developed, her character is important in that she represents what Joan could have become: a working stiff mocked by all who becomes a literal stiff, dying at her desk. Ms. B. had no choices, and once her looks faded, she continued to toil away, and to be the butt of cruel jokes. Ms. B. is Joan's cautionary tale. Joan escapes the same fate by marrying Greg—even if he is prone to devaluing her and treating her as if she is second rate.

THE PSYCHOLOGY OF CAPITALISM

Roger and Don discuss what they want the newest incarnation of Sterling Cooper to be. They have been taken over, and hope to get out of what has turned into a bad business situation—their new British owners have strangled the firm with cutbacks and layoffs, making all the admen miserable, and have sold the ground beneath them yet again. When Don, Roger, and Pete decide to partner with

Lane Pryce to form a new entity, they behave in true capitalist fashion, their egos fully wrapped up in the venture and in the business of making money. During one difficult business decision, Roger jokes that he wants the new company to be "one in which every partner has a summerhouse." For him and the other men, success means partnership in a financially successful venture with their names on the door. They are typical of the era, a time when many boomers saw their fortunes rise in tandem with a strong economy and a positive world outlook.

Many companies were paternalistic toward employees in the *Mad Men* era. Miss Blankenship has been around since the original agency's inception, for example. Likewise, the partners (Bert, Roger, and Don), perhaps the most old-school, are loathe to fire Freddy, though they ultimately have to do so. Then the workplace was a solid, more permanent institution for many individuals. Now workers no longer remain at jobs for an entire career. Many move or have lost jobs due to the economic hardships of late, while others telecommute and do not take part at all in office communities. And years of laissez-faire government policies have allowed finance to go unregulated, enabling the proliferation of transactions involving derivative and synthetic financial products—transactions so complex they are beyond the ken of most, even their participants. We see the beginnings of this greed and lack of corporate loyalty on the show. Don, Peggy, Pete, and others begin to be courted and enjoined to jump to other agencies. Roger wants even more money and displays an attitude akin to "let's grab what we can, and more." These are the precursors to the entitlement and narcissism that have continued to grow unabated. Today no amount of money is ever enough. There is an outsized emphasis on wealth and acquisition.

So, what would Don and Roger's working personas look like in our current times? The Dons of today aim high. They possess the belief that they are special and talented. They take their companies public and splash their faces all over billboards. They franchise their businesses out to different cities. Or they establish their own financial firms and seek outsized profits—their only goal is to amass wealth and power, despite risks or costs to society at large. They do not value or enjoy the intrinsic pursuits of their work.

Many at Sterling Cooper do enjoy the work they do, though. So while we do see the seeds of greed and the beginnings of millennial capitalism in Roger, they do not tell the whole story. Sure, a few of the guys complain about not getting ahead, and a couple of them have a short story in their back pocket and other literary aspirations, but the challenges of their work fuel them and inspire their creativity. Don always hunkers down and churns out a good campaign—and he doesn't seem to mind the hard work. He knows when he has hit a home run, and he enjoys the pitch. Peggy is similar. She sometimes toys with choosing social opportunities over deadlines, but she never does. She finds her work compelling and is proud of her copywriting, contributions, and ability to break through the glass ceiling. Pete shows his admiration for Don's talents, even as he tries to one-up him. He continues to pitch and bring in new clients. He likes the advertising game as well as the others.

4

Sex, Drugs, and Johnnie Walker

Don and Roger can down a bottle of whiskey at their desks, yet they still manage to spin out campaigns and make it to meetings on time. Some of their workplace antics appear downright outrageous by modern standards—scotch at eleven in the morning?—and provide vicarious thrills, even if watching that eighth swig and fifteenth cigarette also leaves us feeling more than a bit nauseated.

It was the '60s, of course; a different era. The admen often appeared to be having a good time, and seemed comfortable at work, a contradiction posed by the show: they were bound by stereotypes, manners, and convention but still felt free to indulge. Today's workers might get away with less confining clothing and comportment (flip-flops and e-mails with emoticons?), but our modern workplaces are not as lenient as Sterling Cooper appears to be.

To our millennial eyes, then, Don's and Roger's use of alcohol is often confusing. Both men go to work every day, do their jobs, pay their bills—how can they do all that and still be alcoholics?

Maybe they are just a couple of macho guys who enjoy drinks and women? Alcoholism was less publicized in 1965, and was not well understood. At Sterling Cooper and firms like it, no one worried about how early, how much, or in front of whom consumption occurred. The admen were known as much for their boozing as for their creative campaigns. Liquid brown was part of Madison Avenue's advertising culture and served as its creative fuel.

Behaviors that were once creative and charming now look alcoholic, though. The amount of imbibing the Mad Men participate in would likely land the present-day Dons and Rogers in psychiatric or substance-abuse facilities. So what has changed since the mid-sixties, and why do workplaces eschew on-the-job consumption? For one, there has been a shift in how alcohol and other substances have come to be viewed by the public and the medical community. Today, alcoholism is better understood. Most treatment professionals view it as a disease, not the moral weakness it was then perceived to be.

This change in attitudes toward addiction reflects, and has possibly even spawned, a generation that is more open and willing to discuss drinking, drugs, and treatment. When adman Freddy Rumson lost control of his bladder, wet his pants, and passed out at his desk in front of the team, Peggy's morning-after advice was, "It's over. There's no reason to talk about it." Clearly, she felt awkward about his drinking and loss of control, and he did not push her to talk (Season 2, Episode 9, "Six Month Leave").

Addiction was a source of shame in Peggy and Freddy's time, to be sure. If treatment was sought, it was called a "rest," hidden as attendance at an "out-of-town work conference," or kept a secret. No more. Today, though some continue to whisper about "problem drinkers" and others hide their struggles with substances in shame, the business of seeking rehab has become commonplace—or glamorous—for many. The presence of celebrities and the wealthy in such facilities gives it a sheen, even as they struggle to overcome their problems just like everyone else. To some, rehab is the new black.

It wasn't always this way. In the late 1930s when Alcoholics Anonymous was founded, treatment facilities were run out of people's homes and were operated by fellowships and staffed by recovering addicts, their families, and other mostly non-medical individuals. Rehab was the successor to the infamous "drunk tanks," the steel encasements in hospitals and jails that resembled prison cells and held overindulgers until they could dry out. It was not until around the time of World War II that facilities for alcoholics were operated by the medical establishment. At this point alcohol addiction began to be seen as a disease—a radical departure from the view that alcoholics are people with a moral weakness who do not choose to get better.

As AA grew, the public and medical profession's awareness of alcohol was raised—and pop culture hopped right on the bandwagon. Movies such as *The Lost Weekend* (1945) and *The Days of Wine and Roses* (1962) began the demystification of alcohol addiction, and public awareness of addictions and substance-abuse disorders continued to grow. Likewise, scientific papers about alcoholism were presented at the American Medical Association, and bolstered understanding in members of the medical profession. By the mid-1970s, AA would have approximately 1 million members and 28,000 groups in over 90 countries worldwide.[1]

All this to say that Don and his 1960s colleagues must have known that drinking at all hours of the day was bad for their health, that it destroyed relationships and wrecked careers, and that some people sought treatment for addiction—yet they do not usually seem to know that their own personal behaviors are alcoholic. Such failure in insight can be explained by two factors, one sociological, one psychological: habituation and denial.

THE PSYCHOLOGY OF ALCOHOLISM

Since boozing was part of the culture of Madison Avenue in the 1960s, those at ad agencies routinely witnessed heavy workplace drinking and understood it to be the norm. In sociological terms, they became "habituated" to watching their coworkers pound drinks. It makes sense; when everyone in the group behaves a certain way, the behavior becomes the norm for the group and is unlikely to raise any eyebrows, even if it is dangerous or unhealthy.

Psychoanalysts wouldn't argue with the fact that one's peer group has a powerful affect on habits and attitudes. But instead of attributing heavy drinking to the process of habituation, they would see it as having to do less with the peer group than with genetics and the personality of the drinker. Viewed in this way, alcoholism involves a difficulty regulating impulses and moods, reflects a tendency to behave in self-defeating ways, and requires denial, just like Peggy's inability to know she is pregnant. In both cases, the need not to see what is really going on is an emotionally generated failure of insight.

Alcoholics and substance abusers frequently deny that their use is destructive, and claim that they can control it. One way to understand this sort of denial is to think of an alcoholic brain as an organism in battle with itself. One side of the brain wants a drink; once it gets one, it demands another, then another. Even as the other side of the brain questions whether having this many drinks is a problem, the drinking continues. The reluctant voice becomes weaker and weaker until it is drowned out by the desire to keep drinking, and by the impulse to feed the addiction. The denial has taken over.

And denial is a potent component of any addiction. It reflects a lack of conscious awareness of one's harmful behaviors, as well as an inability to perceive both the progression of the addiction and the adverse consequences of a substance's continued use. Those who have reservations about the amount of their intake continue to drink because once they start, they lose control and cannot stop.

In addition to denial, those struggling with addictions often use substances for other reasons, such an inability to process, or even tolerate, feelings they cannot bear. So when Don receives a message that his beloved Anna is dying, he drowns himself in booze, unable to handle the pain of her loss. In the instant when his secretary hands him a written phone message, he reaches for the phone, but pours a tall one instead. He continues to drink all night—even after vomiting and having a fistfight with Duck (Season 4, Episode 7, "The Suitcase").

Addicts drink to stem the flood of their feelings and dark moods. They drink to socialize. They drink to celebrate. They drink to deal with the pressures of work. They drink to forget work. And they drink to forget why they are drinking in the first place. Heavy drinking eventually becomes a habit, as natural as your morning coffee or brushing your teeth at night.

Many alcoholics routinely drink in the morning, especially if they feel queasy or under the weather. Those who become emotionally dependent on alcohol feel they cannot get through a difficult situation without a drink. Habitual users may become physically dependent, as well. They need to drink or they will become ill. At the most severe and advanced stages of alcoholism, withdrawal occurs, and can cause uncontrollable physical shaking, anxiety, restlessness, irritability, moodiness, intense cravings for more booze, and, infrequently, hallucinations. In rare cases withdrawing addicts can develop delirium tremens, a dangerous condition that needs to be supervised, as medical complications like seizures can also occur.[2]

1960s MADISON AVENUE: UNDER THE INFLUENCE

Like many in his milieu, Don often starts drinking early in the day. His tolerance seems to grow, and his boozing to progress. Ultimately his personal life begins to unravel, and his drinking becomes more and more out of control. Throughout Don's ascent at Sterling Cooper, he consumes large amounts of alcohol every single day. Is he an alcoholic, though?

In the early years at the agency, Don's day begins with a gorgeous secretary taking his coat and hat and bringing him a steaming mug of coffee. He is prepped on his schedule, meets with his staff, takes calls, and works on client campaigns. By midafternoon he is pouring smoky liquid into a tumbler of ice. Lunches are an important part of the job—and they are a many-drink occasion. Drinks continue to be poured at meetings and client presentations, and again in late afternoon. When Don returns home to Ossining, he indulges even more with Betty. So, is he or isn't he?

There are two facets of alcohol addiction: abuse and dependence. Abuse is characterized by drinking to excess on multiple occasions in episodes or binges. It also involves under-the-influence participation in a dangerous behavior, like driving a vehicle. Dependence involves a daily intake of large amounts of alcohol, the development of a tolerance for it, and a host of other problems, like physical symptoms of withdrawal and blackouts, as well as problems in health, work, and relationships.

Don drives drunk. We've seen him drink for hours at Sardi's with Bobbie, the wife of a performer hired by client Utz potato chips, then take her for a long drive and make-out session. She makes a move and Don loses control while driving, an open bottle of liquor in his lap. When he fails to see an oncoming car, he crashes and ends up at the police station (Season 2, Episode 5, "The New Girl").

Even back then there were those who frowned upon drinking and driving, though. For example, the precinct officer remarks with contempt, "But you did fail the sobriety test. The fine's one hundred and fifty dollars." "What's your problem?" Don snaps. "There could have been kids out on that road," the officer practically spits back. Outside of Madison Avenue, Don's drinking is viewed in darker, more suspect ways. It's not the norm, as Don assumes.

It is not just the men on the show who drink. Betty drinks during the day when she is at her most miserable, and she hides her drinking from her family and friends. Betty's relationship to alcohol is not fully developed, but she seems to abuse it when she is depressed by the breakup of her marriage. Betty's drinking does not appear to spiral, though; once married to Henry she seems mostly to drink at social gatherings, and we do not see her reach the point of intoxication except on the most stressful occasions, such as the time she sees Don out on a date with Bethany Van Nuys. Henry clearly disapproves, though this is not fully developed on the show.

Roger Sterling also abuses alcohol. When he and Don have lunch one afternoon, for example, Roger gorges on liquor, oysters, and cheesecake—all at Don's urging. Don arranges to have the building elevator taken out of service (to get even with Roger for flirting with Betty on a prior occasion). Forced to climb twenty-three flights of stairs to the office, Roger throws up in the firm's reception area, right front of clients (Season 1, Episode 7, "Red in the Face"). Despite what must have been acute humiliation, he continues to smoke cigarettes, drink to excess, and carouse with much younger women after he has a massive heart attack. In the parlance of substance abuse treatment, he continues to use, despite dangerous consequences to his health.

Alcohol abuse, while common, is difficult to understand. Some seem to be able to binge drink until the point of intoxication, with slurring, memory lapses, errors in judgment, and passing out—but the binges happen only infrequently. These individuals *appear* to be functioning at work and at home. For others the pattern is different. They might have binges like Don's (hours or days of heavy drinking) followed by long or short periods of sobriety. If they are mostly sober but binge only a few times a year, and if they hold on to their jobs and relationships, do they really have a problem?

Once a drinker is off and running, if he or she cannot stop, slow down, or cut back despite adverse effects and consequences, mental health professionals would agree that such behavior is tantamount to alcoholism. By these standards Don definitely abuses alcohol. But he does not stop there. His drinking escalates even further. Compare his behavior in the early 1960s, in which he drinks socially and to entertain clients, with his drinking patterns in 1965. By then his drinking has progressed; he does it daily, until the point of passing out on most days. On the day of the Clio awards, Don drinks all day at work and all night. He almost crosses the line at a client meeting early the next morning when he pitches to Life cereal executives while visibly drunk. We see his colleagues look uncomfortable; they seem to be wondering, "How far will he go? Is he out of control? Will he make a fool of himself—and us?" (Season 4, Episode 6, "Waldorf Stories.")

So how come no one sent Don to rehab? One simple answer: alcoholism was culturally accepted. Drinking was what people commonly did in every milieu in which Don found himself—be it socializing at dinner parties with his white Anglo-Saxon Protestant neighbors, or in the advertising game, or in 1950s and '60s bon vivant society. The New York scene was full of supper clubs, dinner theater, bars, dance halls, charity benefits, and debutante balls. Everyone seemed to be swilling whatever, whenever, and always emptying a bottle of something. And no one seemed to object. As long as Don doesn't lose complete control by vomiting or wetting himself in a meeting, life will continue.

Don hits bottom in the period just before Anna Draper's death. He has been close to the real Don's wife for years. Knowing she is ill, he drinks his way through the final days of her illness and the end of her life—while ignoring her niece's calls. He is medicating his feelings because losing Anna is too painful. During this night, Don eventually downs so much whiskey that his system revolts, and he vomits in the men's room and on his shirt. Drunk, sick, and soiled, he brawls with Duck, who has called Peggy a whore. Just after, even though it is the middle of the night, Don pours yet another drink. "How long are you going to go on like this?" Peggy asks before he passes out, head in her lap (Season 4, Episode 7, "The Suitcase").

So given Don's heavy use despite continued adverse consequences, how come Don *seems* to be able to cut down and possibly even stop drinking so easily after Anna dies? In the episode where the viewer is let in on his inner monologue, he thinks silently, "They say as soon as you have to cut down on your drinking, you have a drinking problem." After admitting this to himself, he tries to stop (Season 4, Episode 8, "The Summer Man"). He replaces alcohol consumption with other behaviors, such as swimming and keeping a journal. He sits through his cravings and tries to get healthy. Though he eventually meets the much younger Megan and plans to start fresh with her, he is not in any sort of treatment or engaging in any attempt at overall psychological change. He has not sworn off alcohol, either. Despite his attempts to put the past behind him and move forward, one can speculate that Don will soon be on the same downhill course, unable to control his alcohol intake.

Don, like others who are accustomed to daily doses of alcohol, drinks to control feelings he has on the inside while compulsively spinning his image on the outside. Yet he winds up losing control over both his drinking and his image. Alcoholics like Don are, in AA parlance, control freaks that are, in reality, out of control.

ALCOHOLISM AND CONTROL

Addiction, by definition, involves a loss of control. Addicts lose the ability to pull back from or reflect on their intake. They develop physical cravings. Their situation becomes a paradox; the more they use, the more they need to get through the day. Human emotions that were always difficult become even harder to bear, and many spend their days chasing equanimity—thus they cede control in continued efforts to escape their pain.

Why this loss of control? Two factors explain this: a constitutional basis for addiction and difficulties with emotion regulation in afflicted individuals. Addiction runs in families, is more common in certain cultures than others, and is understood to have a genetic component. It is also a function of difficulties in self-soothing and in the individual's ability to contain feelings and impulses. Problems in the earliest parent-child relationships can contribute to this, and are evident over generations. That is because effective parents teach their youngest infants and children how to deal with their moods and overwhelming feelings. Children learn how to regulate their emotions when their parents model how to do this for them. Plus, they internalize their parents' soothing words and actions over time until they can soothe and calm themselves and handle their own emotions. In some families parents are not around or cannot do this effectively. Unable to self-soothe, such children often grow up to need substances to salve difficult feelings.

FREDDY'S "CONDUCT UNBEFITTING"

Why does Don's and Roger's heavy drinking fly under the radar, while Freddy's causes him to lose his job?

When Freddy wets himself and passes out during a meeting where the team readies a pitch, he has crossed an imaginary line in the sand. And the reactions of those present are varied: Peggy is upset and serious; she worries about Freddy and tries to protect him. Pete says it is "disgusting" (he seems to be of the mind that alcoholism is a moral weakness). Sal, the art director, laughs hysterically (not a drunk himself, he does not judge Freddy for his problem; instead he takes a carefree fraternity boy stance—laughing about what might make others uncomfortable).

Duck is not at the pre-pitch conference, but learns about it from Pete. His reaction is perhaps most interesting. Duck is himself an alcoholic who is dry at the point when Freddy's problems reach a head. He behaves in an opportunistic manner, and goes right for Freddy's jugular, arranging a meeting with Roger, Don and Pete, in which he pushes them to oust Freddy so he can take over his accounts. He has no mercy, no sympathy for Freddy or his struggles with alcohol. "We're not doing him any favors keeping him around," a self-righteous Duck declares when Don protests the firing during the closed-door meeting at which Freddy's future is determined. We can infer that he is harshly judging Freddy for struggling with a problem he also has; one he loathes in himself. Roger makes up his mind to fire him. He calls Freddy's loss of control "conduct unbefitting" (Season 2, Episode 9, "Six Month Leave").

The loss of Freddy's job is a likely impetus for his decision to seek help. He attends AA meetings. And it seems to work—he eventually manages to stay sober, and is ultimately rehired by the agency. He openly discusses his decision to stop drinking and his efforts to stay sober.

The hard data about alcoholism—as evidenced by CT and PET scans—demonstrates that it kills brain cells, specifically those in the mammilary bodies, the region of the brain associated with memory. Some who abuse alcohol over a period of many years have been known to develop wet brain, or Wernicke-Korsakoff syndrome, a permanent condition in which those afflicted are unable to make new memories at all. They become trapped in a permanent past, blithely unaware that it is no longer, say, 1943, and that they are no longer young and virile.

Certainly most people who drink—and even those who drink heavily—don't develop this syndrome, although Roger's irresponsible drinking seems to be a way of trying to hold on to his youth. His hard-partying lifestyle takes its toll on his health and relationship with his first wife, Mona. So why does he keep hitting the bottle? For Roger it seems to be part of the chase; he is on a constant quest for youth and virility. Drinking, going to fancy restaurants and hotels, squiring beautiful younger women around makes Roger feel like a glamorous bon vivant. Every drink, drag of a cigarette, and woman makes him feel more alive—and despite adverse consequences, he needs all of these things, and especially alcohol, to feel good about himself. And he seems to really like the buzz it confers.

He doesn't give up his hard drinking and smoking ways despite their potentially high costs to his physical health and interpersonal relationships.

THE TIMES THEY WERE A-CHANGIN'

Despite the fact that Don and Roger drink their way through much of the 1960s, at some point workplace consumption began to be frowned upon. First, alcoholism came to be better understood and to be viewed as a disease with a genetic component. At the same time, the nation was gripped by a physical fitness movement. *The Jack LaLanne Show* had millions of viewers. Americans jettisoned cigarettes—which were known to cause pulmonary illness and cancer—joined gyms, and sought a healthy lifestyle. By 1981, a sweatband-wearing Olivia Newton John encouraged Americans to "get physical."

But Don doesn't wait for Olivia Newton John. Always ahead of every trend, he is in the vanguard, even if it's by accident. When the government starts to crack down on cigarette advertising, Don sees the future and knows what he must do. Whether it is dumb luck or whether he is a true visionary who sees the changing ethos, Don embraces the health trend—on paper at least. And so, a consistently hard-partying and heavy-smoking Don Draper, without the knowledge or consent of his partners, publicly decries cigarettes and smoking. His *New York Times* ad represents not only a desperate attempt to spin a positive image for the firm, but also a personal grasp at self-salvation (Season 4, Episode 12, "Blowing Smoke").

Prior to his resolve to get healthy, Don's forward-thinking ways had led him to experiment with marijuana, even before its use became more widespread. By the latter part of the 1960s, the counterculture drug movement was thriving in the United States. Substances other than booze grew in popularity—pot, some uppers and downers, and other pills came onto the scene. Though the counterculture was drugging, mainstream society was becoming more and more conservative in its thinking and behaviors. The two were about to clash in a major cultural explosion.

During Don's time, the country and the world experienced radical changes and enormous social, political, and cultural unrest. First there were the beatniks, and then the hippies—many of whom advocated for substances like pot and LSD, as they believed drugs expanded the mind. The hippie culture of "flower power," love-ins, and sit-ins began in a peaceful enough way, but quickly progressed to anger and unrest—and all within a few years. Whereas the sex, drugs, and rock 'n' roll at Woodstock were violence-free, the Weathermen, Vietnam, the Black Panthers, politically driven public assassinations, and Watergate were soon to arrive on the scene. At this point the nation was rocked by anger and rebellion. The children of the aging hard-drinking admen and -women preferred marijuana to liquor, and booze lost popularity.

"GOT TO GET YOU INTO MY LIFE": MARIJUANA

Around the time Don was winning a Clio, the Beat generation was still hanging around in coffee shops, apartments, and parks throughout Greenwich Village. Led by Allen Ginsberg, they smoked pot regularly, and claimed the drug opened their minds.

Martin Booth, author of *Cannabis: A History*, describes the popularity of pot. "In the mid-1960s . . . half the population was under the age of thirty and agitated, alienated from its elders . . . Marijuana was the battle flag of this cultural upheaval . . . For those who chose this alternative to materialistic, mundane America, it delivered emancipation the like [sic] of which they could never have dreamed."[3]

In the era just preceding Don's, then, many in mainstream society associated marijuana with lethargy, moral turpitude, and the lower echelons of society. Immigrants and African-Americans had used it before World War II, as had musicians during the height of the jazz age. Movies like *Reefer Madness* (1936) had employed fear tactics to convince the generation of men and women before Don and Betty that marijuana was dangerous and evil.

When Don has an affair with Midge Daniels, who lives in Greenwich Village, they consort with poets, artists, and Ginsberg followers, all of whom make clear their distrust of businessmen like Don, representatives of corporate America. Don laughs Midge's friends off, but he joins them in smoking pot at her apartment. When the police come, he manages to walk out of the apartment without incident. Even though he, too, has smoked pot, no one bothers him because he appears to be respectable in his gray flannel suit and hat (Season 1, Episode 8, "The Hobo Code").

He doesn't seem to like marijuana that much. Despite his maverick ways, Don seems to feel like a hypocrite for indulging in the hippie drug. His loosened state and feelings that he is not all what he purports to be give him flashbacks to his own childhood and to his hypocritical stepmother, who held herself out as a good Christian but treated him unkindly and with disdain, and his father, who failed to pay a hardworking down-on-his-luck hobo as promised but made sure to say grace before meals. After smoking pot, Don feels disillusioned with his current life and rushes home to wake Bobby, promising him, "I will never lie to you."

Peggy also tries pot, first at the office with Paul and his buddy, and later with her friend Joyce and her group of artists and journalists. Peggy's secretary confronts her about getting high (nice girls didn't do such things!), but Peggy dresses her down. She has a job and doesn't need anyone's advice. This is the first rumbling of Peggy's rebellion against social prescriptions for good girls. She continues to push the envelope by hanging around with Joyce and her friends, and becomes involved with a young reporter who makes her question Sterling Cooper's 1960s-era attitudes. Pot is in plentiful supply among the members of Joyce's gang. It was a popular choice for many—in fact, some commentators thought that the Beatles were referring to it in their hit song "Got to Get You into My Life."

Years after Midge's affair with Don, she shows up in the lobby of the Sterling Cooper office building and we see the toll her drug use has taken. Midge has progressed from marijuana to heroin. Looking much worse for the wear, she tries to seduce Don in the hope that he will buy one of her paintings. Though Midge is no longer sexually appealing to Don, he writes her a check out of pity (Season 4, Episode 12, "Blowing Smoke"). Seeing how Midge's bohemian, drug-fueled life has turned out scares Don. He has tried living as a bachelor in the Village, and finds that the more conventional life he was constantly fleeing with Betty is starting to look appealing once more. He runs back to a traditional existence with the conservative and safe Megan. His bachelor experiment in the Village seems to have failed, and he decides to get healthy and later to embrace the type of lifestyle he once had with Betty and the kids.

Drugs are not Don's preferred means of self-anesthetizing. If, as Booth claims, drugs "raise the battle flag of rebellion," Don does not really need them or feel the urge to stick it to conventional society—he feels comfortable and thrives in traditional settings. He is part of the establishment and looks down on the counterculture. Instead of thumbing his nose at authority, he joins and ascends the hierarchy. Though he has lived in the Village among artists, Beatniks, and single people, he does not aggressively attack society's rules; he channels his aggression and turns it into a relentless workaholism. While Don prefers hard liquor to drugs, it seems likely his children will grow up to experiment with them, given the time in history at which they will come of age. Betty has already caught Sally smoking a cigarette—pot will surely not be far behind in a few years' time.

5
Sexism and Misogyny

In her 1969 novel *The Edible Woman*, Margaret Atwood claims that females have been relegated to menial jobs and subservient roles, used by men, and valued for their looks. Her heroine, an initially nameless reader of market research surveys, becomes engaged to handsome lawyer Peter, and coworkers are admiring and envious—he provides an escape hatch from their dead-end gig and sexist boss. But Peter does not emotionally engage; after sex he perches his ashtray on top of his fiancée's naked body. Feeling lost and objectified, she bakes him a girlie-shaped cake, adorned with lush lips and ornate lashes. Atwood's point: all men really want is an object to gratify their needs.

Though a fictional work, the novel is set in the real world, and offers a dystopian vision of 1960s attitudes—in the workplace and after hours. It also bears some similarity to the events portrayed on *Mad Men*. For back then most women were like Joan: stuck in administrative positions, and seen as sex objects. Marriage, even to an insensitive clod, was viewed as a way out, the key to an enviable existence.

Certainly there were some who had begun to break the gender mold—there were researchers and copy editors at magazines and newspapers, and there were copywriters at advertising agencies. But ascendency to such positions was achieved and won only through long and hard-fought battles. The women of the era were almost always hired to fill an administrative need. Those who made it past the secretarial level to professional positions had struggled to do so.

Employers and institutions were hardly family friendly. With no possibility of maternity leave, most women were encouraged to stop working when they had their first baby. Women who worked or trained for careers were viewed as competing with men, and as taking jobs that rightly belonged to them—so much so that men's and women's job listings were posted on separate pages in male and female sections of the want ads. Women could work as typists, secretaries, nurses, social workers, or stewardesses. Other professional positions were reserved for men, who were viewed as having families to support.

There were precious few female role models for working women at this time, either. According to *New York Times* journalist Gail Collins, who interviewed scores of women for her book *When Everything Changed: The Amazing Journey of American Women from 1960 to the Present*, female mentors and role models were virtually nonexistent in most organizations and institutions of the time. One sociologist she spoke with, Jo Freeman, who had studied at Berkeley for years, remarked that she had never even seen a woman professor there—nor did she even notice this gap at the time.[1] Women who came of age during the 1950s and '60s did not expect much in terms of opportunity, advancement, legal protection, or mentoring.

As History and Family Studies Professor Stephanie Coontz, codirector of the Council on Contemporary Families, makes clear in her book *A Strange Stirring: The Feminine Mystique and American Women at the Dawn of the 1960s*, the common goal of most young women of the time was to get married and have a family. Married women could have careers until kids came along—as long as their earnings didn't eclipse their husbands'. A woman who discovered she was outearning her husband frequently decided to switch to a lesser-paying job and take a cut in income, so as to preserve his status as breadwinner—and his self-esteem.[2]

Mothers who worked were seen as shirking child- and home-care responsibilities. Those who had personal or career ambitions were viewed with suspicion. And since personal ambition was hidden, a source of shame, it was natural for women to defer to their husbands in most matters. When Betty Draper wants to work as a print model, she asks Don for permission to take the job (Season 1, Episode 9, "Shoot").

Likewise, it is ultimately Don's decision to let Betty and the children remain in the house after the divorce. The home was his property, not hers. Women at that time had no legal rights or claims to marital property. In most states if a couple divorced and the wife had been a homemaker she was not entitled to share her husband's earnings.[3]

Medical doctors of the time were sexist and demeaning in their view and treatment of female patients. Females were routinely seen as "hysterical," and too emotional to give consent for their own medical procedures. Physicians consulted with husbands behind patients' backs, and made decisions about the nature and course of treatment.[4] We see Betty's psychiatrist, Dr. Wayne, break confidentiality in order to fill Don in on session content. "I had a very interesting hour with your wife today," he says (Season 1, Episode 2, "Ladies Room"). And when Betty opens the phone bill, which is addressed only to Mr. Donald Draper, she learns that Don has been discussing her with her doctor behind her back. She looks crushed to discover this betrayal, but she does not confront Dr. Wayne in their next session. Instead, she tells him that she would be happier if her husband did not cheat on her, and hopes it will get back to Don. Indirect suggestions and attempts at manipulation are the only forms of power and payback Betty has (Season 1, Episode 13, "The Wheel").

In a call with Don, Dr. Wayne shows a condescending attitude toward women when he describes Betty as "having the emotions of a child" (Season 1, Episode 7, "Red in the Face"). During their sessions he remains quiet, even after Betty tells him several times that her mother has recently died. It was a common practice at the time for the analyst to remain almost totally silent during most sessions, but his almost cartoonish adherence to textbook ideals appears rejecting and lacking in empathy by contemporary standards.

Wayne's patronizing attitude toward his female patients reflects the era's view that a woman with a husband, children, and a lovely home had it all. If she felt any sort of dissatisfaction or lack of fulfillment, she was at fault. If she was sad or uneasy, it meant she had a problem. Physicians in branches of medicine other than psychiatry were generally no different than Dr. Wayne.

Betty is, in fact, constantly told by those around her that she "has everything": her Grace Kelly looks seem to provide the means to a perfect life. Her classic features and blond hair allow her to model, and attract the handsome and upwardly mobile Don. But, as we know, the Drapers' marriage soon becomes an unhappy one, and Betty's looks fail her; she is powerless to bridge the growing distance between herself and her spouse. She feels increasingly bored and disaffected. Her beauty seems more like a curse that confines her to live in a modern-day Gothic prison—only she is trapped in a lonely Westchester colonial, instead of in a forbidding stone castle. The future looks dark, until Betty's gorgeous appearance plays another role in her destiny. Since she has been taught that looks represent her only possible currency, she keeps them fresh—and is soon rewarded with an escape. Betty finds another man to marry, though it seems clear that their initial attraction will also wear thin, leaving her to feel trapped and miserable yet again.

Things are not much better for Joan. Her fiancé, himself a physician, is also controlling and devaluing in his attitudes toward women. He forces her to have sex against her will, even though she says no at least three different times when he pushes her down. Joan marries him anyway. Being married to a sexist cad and a rapist is obviously preferable to becoming the office spinster, like Ida Blankenship. Choices for women were few and far between. For those who did not marry at all, the future was grim.

More on Joan and the others later, but first, back to Betty.

LONELY BETTY

Betty, a college graduate, works briefly as a model before being wooed by Don. Once married, she has two children. As Don's financial fortunes rise, Betty has more and more time on her hands, and fewer ways to occupy it.

To Don, Betty's role is clear cut: she is a mother and a housewife. At first she tries to be the perfect wife and hostess. On one occasion Betty throws an elegant around-the-world dinner party for another couple. The husband, Crab Colson, works in the advertising field as well, and the men discuss business at the Drapers' gathering. In fact, Betty serves Heineken and Don points out that this choice is in line with market research. After the guests leave, Betty is furious at being treated as a research subject, and accuses Don of humiliating her and behaving selfishly.

Their angry exchange is clearly not just about beer. Betty feels devalued, and betrayed by her husband. She has made a huge effort to be perfect for Don, but he has taken advantage of her, she feels, and has degraded her by using her consumer preferences to make a point with colleagues. Even worse, he has cheated on her. She's apparently known that he was unfaithful for some time, but a recent call from Jimmy Barrett has made her realize that everyone else knows it, too. Like Don, Betty can convince herself that all is well as long as other people believe that to be the case. The beer is the last straw—Don's womanizing has made her feel invisible, marginalized, and unimportant for far too long. It is the beginning of the end of their marriage (Season 2, Episode 8, "A Night to Remember").

As a housewife, Betty is expected to serve her husband and entertain his guests. She is not expected to think independently, have separate interests, or possess a discrete identity. She is not permitted to develop any aspects of herself outside of the wife and mothering functions. Her life is one of confinement and limitations, and she isn't really allowed to be a person who functions out in the world.

As Betty's role becomes more and more binding and unsatisfying, she turns to Don for attention. His fear of intimacy and abandonment makes him a less than ideal partner, to say the least. Betty feels cast off and humiliated, and their marriage falls apart. Her decision to throw her husband out is an attempt to take back a small measure of power in the only way available to her.

For Betty does not have much power at all. Pampered and bored, she doesn't enjoy herself in the suburbs. Her mother dies, and like many who have lost a parent, Betty begins to feel sad, lost, and lonely. At the same time, her husband becomes distant. During his affair with Rachel Menken, he turns down Betty's offers of sex. He'd rather read in bed than be intimate. She begins to feel more and more isolated, anxious, and sad. She also grows apart from her children as they age and take on separate identities beyond her control.

Betty becomes bitter and immobilized as all of her relationships go sour. She tries to make a home and family. She finds it unsatisfying and empty. She tries to please her husband but cannot make him happy. She is cold and quietly angry much of the time—unless she is berating one of her children—because she has been raised to hide emotions. Instead of showing what she feels, she freezes up and draws inward, a strategy that causes her to feel even more despondent. While she passively accepts the circumstances of her life, including a bland life in the suburbs and fractious relationships with Don and the children (especially her daughter), she feels increasingly hopeless, but she lacks the energy or motivation to change anything, becoming more and more depressed because she cannot see any way out of her dead-end situation. On some days she wears a housecoat and doesn't interact with anyone, even her children. Sometimes she drinks to numb the pain; other times she sleeps most of the day.

Betty feels she has been burned by those close to her, and she does not want to be hurt anymore. So, she simply stops trying. The loss of personal motivation, rise in feelings of entrapment, and apathy that develop after a series of disappointments is an emotional state known to psychologists as "learned helplessness."

Disappointed and browbeaten, Betty has become more and more listless—until she finds an escape hatch, and only then can she take action. She meets and decides to marry Henry Francis, a wealthy older man. With this turn of events, her role as wife and mother is affirmed, and her vision narrowed even further—it's not her life that's the problem, she just had the wrong man! An identity as someone's wife is the only existence imaginable for Betty.

The only other avenues she's observed—a single mother working a sad menial job, like Helen Bishop, or a "party girl" like her friend Juanita, whom Don and Betty see with an unattractive older man at the Savoy—are not at all appealing to her. Psychologically, Henry serves as a "transformational object" for Betty; one that she hopes will change the course of her life forever, rescue her, and fix her problems for her. But this type of metamorphosis is a pipe dream. Betty sees the fix as coming from the outside. She does not focus on her mental state, and she is not reflective. Rather, she wants to be taken care of and loved, and does not aspire to solve her own problems. She wants someone else to change her life for her.

While marrying a knight in shining armor and hoping for a major transformation is a common dream for many young girls and women, those who expect someone else to fix their lives for them frequently wind up feeling disappointed. Emotional dilemmas and personal struggles are best addressed by figuring out how to understand and change unproductive patterns, not by altering something external. By comparison, Joan and Peggy, though different in their respective approaches to difficult situations, are examples of women who look inward in some ways and attempt to use an internal path to bring about external change and emotional satisfaction.

Despite her beautiful exterior and comfortable life, Betty feels empty emotionally. She suffers from a narcissistic vulnerability, such that she is insecure, takes things personally (her daughter's emotional problems anger her, for example), and needs constant bolstering from the outside. She seeks the attention of men and hopes to be shored up and saved by them. When faced with difficult situations, she crumbles; she does not forge on, as Peggy and Joan do when they are confronted by adverse circumstances.

Betty's psychology and actions are in large part a result of living during an era in which women had few choices. In the early part of the 1960s women could marry and have a family, they could become secretaries, stenographers, or typists, or, if they went to college, they could work as teachers or nurses. Women who pursued a career often had to give up other pursuits, such as marriage or family. Betty's being able to "stay home" confers a degree of social status on the Drapers—it signifies that Don earns enough to support his wife and children in an enviable fashion. But, thus situated, Betty is limited in her options. She is confined to lunching with friends, volunteering for local causes, and shuttling her children back and forth.

According to Germaine Greer, author of *The Female Eunuch*, a wife like Betty "is the dead heart of the family . . . the best thing that can happen is that she can take up again where she left off and go back to work at a job which was only a stopgap when she began it; she can expect no promotion, no significant remuneration, no widening of her horizons. Her work becomes a hypnotic. She cleans, she knits, she embroiders."[5]

Greer views the lot of 1960s housewife as a grim one. She views housewives like Betty as emblematic of the loneliness and despair experienced by women who were constrained by rigid gender roles, scant opportunity, and increasing distance from their spouses. Betty develops a transient inability to use her hands, once even losing control of her car with the kids in tow. When it is determined that her symptom has no neurological basis, only a psychological one, Don reluctantly sends her to a psychiatrist.

HISTRIONIC AND HYSTERICAL PERSONALITY DISORDER, THEN AND NOW

In Freud's day, and for many years thereafter, hysterical ailments were understood to be the result of repressed sexual impulses and anxieties that were forbidden and could not be expressed, acted upon, or remembered; they could only be experienced symptomatically, as paralysis, anxiety, or breathlessness, to name a few examples. A woman's pent-up sexual energy was thought to be the cause of her psychiatric distress. One malady, "glove paralysis" (occurring in one or both hands, and with no underlying neurological basis), was attributed to repressed sexual impulses, and to guilt about masturbating.

Oddly enough, Betty develops a similar type of paralysis. She loses fine motor control in her hands. And she has touched herself on the fainting couch. Though we do not know the cause of Betty's shaking hands, we can easily imagine what the Father of Psychoanalysis might have surmised about this turn of events.

Today, though, Betty's problems with her hands would be understood as a conversion symptom, so named because the disturbance arises when unacceptable emotions are unconsciously converted into something physical. While paralysis with no neurological basis is rarely seen today, somatic complaints (aches and pains with no medical basis, or the persisting conviction that one is dying, despite repeated medical assurances to the contrary) are common. Such ailments fall under the rubric of somatoform disorders.

During Freud's time and for years thereafter, the presence of a single conversion symptom was usually all it took before professionals characterized the sufferer as a hysteric or as suffering from hysterical personality disorder. Today, histrionic personality disorder, the heir apparent to hysterical personality, serves as an umbrella term to describe individuals with somatic and conversion symptoms, as well as a host of other personality traits.

When given, the diagnosis of histrionic personality disorder refers to someone (generally a woman) who is emotional, impressionistic, dramatic, and easily overcome by affects, and who acts seductively—especially at times and in situations when it is inappropriate, such as with doctors or employers.

Two factors explain why mental health disorders are viewed and classified differently today: the nature and type of illnesses seen by mental health professionals has changed, and our methods of understanding psychopathology have evolved since Freud's time. People are now understood in terms of, and treated for, an overall psychological makeup (for example, a long-standing pattern of behavior, such as the tendency to engage in persistent self-defeating actions). Individuals are no longer classified according to a single isolated conversion symptom (like paralysis with no neurological basis). Many also seek and receive help for disturbances of mood such as anxiety and depression. (A note to the reader who may find concepts of classification and diagnosis to be overly dense and somewhat confusing—they are! A discussion of one view of the changing nature of pathology can be found in chapter 2, "The Culture of Narcissism." An explanation of the differences between overall personality makeup and individual symptoms appears in "Psychoanalytic Psychology 101").

Our thinking about conversion symptoms has evolved in other ways since Freud's time. When bodily complaints with no medical or neurological basis are exhibited, they are no longer viewed as sexual in nature; rather, as in Betty's case, they represent an expression of an individual's repeated attempts to find love and to feel cared about. (An aside for those who enjoy an even finer level of precision: modern analysts also make another distinction between the old way of viewing hysteria (it's just sexual energy that has nowhere to go) and the current one: many today would understand Betty's plight as a fusion of her sexual desires and her aggressive impulses. In other words, she has sexual feelings, but no one to sleep with. She is not comfortable with masturbating either. She has aggressive feelings, but was raised not to show them. So she is left with a jumble of unconscious shameful sexual desire and aggression that get fused together and driven inward). Back to the related explanation for Betty's struggles: They are the result of her longing for love and conviction that the way to get it is to be lacking in competence.

During her sessions with the psychiatrist, Betty reflects on her situation. Though her doctor is critical and views her in a narrow way—she is "childlike," "consumed by petty jealousies," and overwhelmed with everyday activities (Season 1, Episode 7, "Red in the Face")—when Betty muses, it becomes apparent that she has developed emotional pain to compensate for a series of losses and for an internal feeling of emptiness.

Modern psychoanalysts would see Betty as someone who unconsciously becomes helpless and incapable because she feels alone and insecure and fears being a competent adult. Such individuals worry that being competent and self-sufficient is tantamount to winding up alone, with no one to take care of them. It is not a coincidence that Betty's hands go numb and she loses control over her car just after seeing a divorced neighbor (Season 1, Episode 2, "Ladies' Room"). On an unconscious level, Betty worries that if she functions too well, Don might leave. Her parents gave her the message that being incompetent and taken care of is tantamount to being loved, and this has become ingrained in her mind, a part of the way she sees herself and her place in the world. While she sometimes feels degraded by Don, being isolated and coddled makes her feel cared for—and this fits in with her version of marital love.

Betty continues to talk to her psychiatrist, and eventually her shaking and loss of muscular control recede. But her loneliness and desperation do not. Terrified of her inner life, she repeatedly acts on impulse so she does not have to feel afraid and alone. Betty defines herself as, and has built her entire existence around being, Mrs. Draper—if she loses Don, what else would she have? Thoughts of sex with other men threaten Betty's identity. So when she fantasizes about an air-conditioning salesman, or encourages her friend Sarah Beth to interact with an engaged man at the riding stables, her actions seem like practice before taking action. She does not readily commit adultery. But after these attempts or "mental trial and error," she does impulsively sleep with a stranger to subvert her awareness of the growing tension and distance between herself and Don (Season 2, Episode 13, "Meditations in an Emergency"). Betty only cheats on that one occasion, though, and remains unhappily married to Don for many months after her foray into infidelity.

Eventually, though, Betty finds a way to extricate herself from her unhappy marriage. She meets Henry Francis, a kind, prominent, older man, and begins an emotional affair with him. Within weeks of meeting him she accepts his proposal of marriage. He becomes her protector and her rescuer (Season 3, Episode 13, "Shut the Door. Have a Seat"). She has no other way to escape her loneliness or gender position—she is both product and victim of her time. If men could shape their destinies through personal and professional accomplishments, marriage was the primary option available for women. According to social psychologists and evolutionary theory, when a married Betty flirts with Henry (and others before him) her behaviors can be understood as biologically driven. She is keeping an eye out for alternative partners, seeking to have a backup mate on the shelf in order to fulfill her biological imperative of reproducing, should anything happen to Don. Her instinct to create an insurance plan also speaks to the weakness of her marriage bond. When Don angrily accuses her of "building a life raft" after he discovers the existence of Henry, he's entirely right.

JOAN'S GLASS CEILING

Joan, like Betty, is confined by her gender, but she is not cowed by setbacks, and does not become helpless in the face of difficulty. Life has not always been easy for Joan. Though she runs the day-to-day operations of the agency, and though she is extremely competent and professional, being female limits her progression. When she does receive an opportunity to review scripts and place advertisements for clients of the agency, her progress is soon thwarted.

All of the men in her orbit seem to see her in only one way: as a supportive presence there to serve them and meet their needs. She is either a mommy or a sex object, the only two possible roles for women during this era. When Joan appears hurt, frustrated, angry, or disappointed, she silences herself. She generally chooses not to challenge the men's stereotypes, or their notions of proper gender role behaviors.

When Joan's fiancé reminds her that her job is to eat "bonbons"—unless he needs her to serve him water or set the table—she handles his devaluing attitude quietly and with humor. She assures him she's enjoying herself, and then quickly jumps up to do his bidding. Her actions say, in effect: "Indulge me; let me have my fun with this, and I promise to never let it interfere. My job is to be your wife first and foremost because your needs are paramount." Though her fiancé wants to keep his wife as a beautiful trophy who jumps up to meet his needs, he grudgingly allows Joan to amuse herself—as long as her pursuits don't jeopardize his interests.

Roger's treatment of Joan is perhaps the most sexist of all. He and Joan share a connection; he seems to care very deeply for, and possibly even love, her. He does not stop to think about her as a separate individual, however, or as a person who exists outside of and apart from his needs. He buys her a fluttering tiger finch as if to say she is his beautiful caged bird that is preserved for his exclusive access—no more, no less. With her trademark shrewd wit, Joan nails his objectification, saying, "If you had your way, I'd be stranded in some paperweight with my legs stuck in the air" (Season 1, Episode 6, "Babylon").

Roger's inability to view Joan as a separate person is due to his narcissistic preoccupations and limitations—he is simply unable to see that there is another human being in the interaction. He cannot look outside of himself to see past the precise nature of his own needs. But Roger is not just psychologically limited. He is clearly stuck in 1950s perceptions of acceptable gender roles. It would never occur to him to think in visionary or iconoclastic ways. To him, Joan is a gorgeous and sexy woman. That means, she is someone to sleep with, and she remains an office administrator, her sole role to make life as easy as possible for the men of the office.

So what does it say about Joan psychologically that she fails to stick up for herself when she is replaced by a man? One explanation is that after being constantly devalued and demoted she has come to share the view that women are second-class. She does not have the self-esteem to demand equal treatment because she is told every day that women are less competent than men and inferior to them. Under these conditions it becomes difficult for her to hold on to a belief that she can succeed at a higher professional level. Joan's plight provides a subtle example of what happens when someone is repeatedly subjected to emotional abuse. The abused person can begin to buy in to the abuse—just as Joan develops a somewhat browbeaten mentality and begins to believe the criticisms and denigrating comments leveled at her and fails to object when men act in sexist ways toward her.

Another explanation for Joan's tendency to take sexist treatment is one that highlights another important theme of the show: can we ever live up to our ideals? Joan has to resolve an internal dilemma involving the different parts of herself; namely, what she wants versus what is expected of her. While she would like to be respected and treated equally, she is given the message that she is second-class and is frequently held back. She lives at a time when most women will never be allowed to realize their potential. She has to come up with a way to reconcile her desires for more with the realities of her situation. She learns to take what she can get, and winds up with a job she likes and a husband she loves, even if neither represents her ideal. This ability to accept limitations imposed by society and make peace with them allows Joan to effectively resolve her internal dilemmas.

It is also possible that Joan refuses to make waves because she is more comfortable in "female" roles like office manager and wife. And in fact, she focuses on getting married and starting a family. Though Greg, her fiancé, forces her to have intercourse against her will (Season 2, Episode 12, "The Mountain King"), and though she knows that he can be devaluing and controlling, she goes through with the wedding. Her behavior after being raped by her fiancé shows how badly she wants to get married and have a husband. She doesn't expect any better treatment, and latching onto a successful man, even if he treats her body as his property, is the only option she has. Likewise, when she finds herself pregnant by Roger and he expects her to get an abortion, she informs him that she will go alone for the procedure and, when there, decides not to terminate the pregnancy. Once again Joan has chosen to do what she wants: keep the baby and pass it off as Greg's. This is who Joan is—she generally manages, even if through subterfuge, to obtain the outcome she desires, whatever the obstacles in her path. She perseveres and comes out ahead, despite adversity.

One could say that Joan is someone who displays psychological health and well-being. She has attained a measure of balance in life. She likes many aspects of her job and succeeds in establishing and maintaining true friendships. For instance, she shares a bond with her roommate, Carol. They talk openly about many things, even though they do not discuss Carol's sexuality. Joan also has true intimacy with Roger, and cares for him despite his flaws, seeing beyond his sexist, racist, demeaning comments, and understanding that his arrogant attitude and humor are covering up his frailty and fear of aging. Their friendship is genuine. Likewise, Joan seems to share a true connection with her husband, Greg. She is distraught when he leaves for the army. They have intimate talks and laugh together on the phone when he is at basic training.

Psychologically, then, Joan does not seem to behave in self-defeating ways, and she chooses to set goals that she can attain. And while she is subject to the limitations of a glass ceiling at work, Joan seems to think about the future and to be able to bring about outcomes she envisions: a job, marriage, and a pregnancy. In this way Joan is more in charge of her personal destiny than Betty.

But if Joan's business fortunes are stymied, those of her coworker, Peggy, are on an upswing.

PEGGY'S CHOICE

Unlike Joan, Peggy manages to work her way out of the secretarial pool. It isn't easy, though.

Everyone in the office hits on Peggy when she reports to work her first week; she is ogled and even kissed by Paul Kinsey against her will. The actions of the all-male group of admen begin to take on a life of their own. This happens all the time; when groups form they become new entities whose emotions exist more intensely—and have a greater impact—than those of individuals. Groups act and think differently, and members can develop a herd mentality, as anyone who has ever studied social psychology or been to a college fraternity party can attest.

Psychoanalytic group theory provides an explanation for the behavior of the all-male creative team. When several individuals develop a shared attitude or a common idea toward someone, the person on the receiving end is slapped with, and has to metabolize, an intense jangle of affects known as a group projection. This is all a fancy way of saying that such a person has a lot to deal with.

Which brings us to Peggy: one cannot help but wonder how she felt when confronted by the parade of men who ogled and objectified her. She is able to withstand their derogatory treatment but does express dismay that she is always "the dessert." Joan tauntingly tells her she should enjoy the attention while it lasts, because she isn't much. Though Peggy feels objectified by the men's devaluing and sexist comments and behaviors, she hides it well. She keeps her anger and discomfitting feelings to herself; it is what she has been taught to do, and it is the way she believes she will succeed—for now.

As long as she's not on the receiving end of the sexism, in fact, Peggy does not seem to fight it in the first few seasons. On the contrary, she aligns herself with the men in the office as a way of protecting herself and negotiating the difficult office landscape (psychoanalysts call this unconscious set of mental gymnastics a defense). Freud first wrote about how a person "identifies" by acting aggressively with another who has treated him or her in a hostile fashion. His daughter, Anna Freud, called this process "identification with the aggressor." She and others who wrote about it have noted that it explains how a victim can act abusively after being treated in similar fashion by a perpetrator of abuse.[6] This explains a lot about Peggy's behavior at work. After being treated like a peon by the men, Peggy immediately turns her own aggression on Lois, another secretary, making her cry by dressing her down about her inappropriate conduct as Don's assistant (Season 2, Episode 1, "For Those Who Think Young"). When she puts Lois in her place, it is a first step in her move toward becoming more assertive (even aggressive)—like the men who have kept her back, at least for the time being. Women's ill treatment of other women at work can be seen as an expression of Peggy's type of identifying with the hostility of the males in positions of power.

Peggy receives advice from Bobbie Barrett, a former dancer who has come up in the world the hard way, through a combination of hard work, using her assets, and being opportunistic. She tells Peggy to act like an equal if she wants the corner office, in effect instructing her to "be a woman," which, as she notes, is "a powerful business when done correctly." Peggy takes Bobbie's advice. The next morning at work she boldly addresses Don by his first name, much to his surprise (Season 2, Episode 5, "The New Girl").

Peggy's ambitions allow her to put her job and career first. She is not at Sterling Cooper to land a husband. Though Peggy works hard at her job and puts her career before her personal life, traditional attitudes toward women still prevail, and she is viewed with suspicion and criticism. When Don does try to give her more responsibility, Pete is overtly hostile and feels threatened (Season 1, Episode 13, "The Wheel").

Peggy does well on the job and moves forward, but she does stumble at times. At one point she is unsure whether sleeping with her boyfriend would ruin her chances of getting him to marry her. She discusses this with Freddy when they write copy for Pond's cold cream, and he protectively and paternally advises her against premarital sex. "He won't respect you" (Season 4, Episode 2, "Christmas Comes but Once a Year").

When writing copy, though, Peggy quickly distinguishes herself at the agency. She and the other secretaries are asked to participate in a focus group for a lipstick client. The men watch for entertainment from behind a two-way mirror—they laugh at the women as if they are exotic zoo animals of a different, inferior species. Even so, Peggy catches Freddy's eye by nailing a pitch in an inventive way. Her hard work and talents impress Don, Freddy, and Ken. But even as he advocates for her, Freddy puts her down. In describing her he tells Don, "It was like watching a dog play the piano" (Season 1, Episode 6, "Babylon"). Despite such sexist overtones, Peggy is promoted to a junior copywriter position. We do not know whether Don's vote of confidence in Peggy is based solely on her accomplishments or if it also serves as his way of taunting Pete. Either way, Pete continues to resent Peggy's presence on the creative team.

It is unclear whether Pete resents having a woman put on the account he has brought in because he is sexist or because he does not want to work in close proximity to Peggy, given his sexual attraction to her—or both.

What *is* clear is that once Peggy enters the new office and all it symbolizes, she has exited the secretarial pool for good. Peggy's psychological style is a work-oriented and -driven one. Individuals who focus on work to the exclusion of everything else, clamping down on feelings, can be said to be obsessional in their character. Obsessional individuals do not necessarily have obsessions, ruminations, or recurring thoughts common to OCD (obsessive-compulsive disorder); rather, they are interpersonally very controlled, are restricted in emotional range, and habitually hold back their anger. Many workaholics fall into this category. Like Peggy, they are organized around achievement, and focus on their jobs to the exclusion of all else. Their personal lives can become almost nonexistent.

JOAN AND PETE'S ENVY

Clearly, Joan needs to put Peggy in her place. But why is she so threatened by her? She can't help but be envious of Peggy.

Envy can be distinguished from jealousy. Though both are powerful emotions, jealousy is known to involve a triangle: the jealous person, the one who is the object of jealousy, and a third party who is experienced as competition by the jealous party. For example, an older sibling might be jealous of the mother's time with a new baby. There are three in the picture, and one is getting in the way of the other.

With envy, though, there are always just two involved. When someone is envious, that person often wants what the other person has—and wants it badly enough to try to grab it away, or do whatever becomes necessary to get it. Envy is felt in a powerful way, and on a deep level; it is not always conscious. The person who is envious feels threatened. He or she covets what the other person has—sometimes to the point of having destructive feelings for the other.

It comes as no surprise that Joan would attempt to knock down Peggy as she rises up, and that Joan would devalue Peggy's copywriting opportunity and belittle her achievements and talents. She envies Peggy, who has succeeded in creating opportunities for herself in the very same situations in which Joan cannot. When envy is malignant enough it is associated with wishes for destruction; meaning, a coworker who believes he is entitled to something another has (say, a promotion), might go to extremes to ruin the envied person's reputation and career. Envy is color- and gender-blind; almost everyone feels it at one time or another, and Joan is no exception. It is only viewed as a problem by mental health professionals when it rises to a destructive level, such that it is deeply shameful to or threatens the envious individual's psychological equilibrium (as we have seen to be the case with other intense emotions that can feel jarring and overwhelming).

Joan's envy does not rise to these levels, though. She is not vengeful; rather, she seems to enjoy minor put-downs and jibes. Her actions are mostly to be taken in the service of consolidating her power, not destroying Peggy's ascent.

Pete's feelings toward Peggy are more complicated, however. He wants Peggy in a sexual way. His attraction is powerful and visceral. Though he tries to ignore his feelings, he cannot. In a sense he can be said to be envious of Peggy's sexuality and freedom as a single woman. He is certainly critical and devaluing when she celebrates her success at P. J. Clarke's by dancing with some of the men from the agency. When she is gliding around doing the twist, Pete sneers, "I don't like you like this" (Season 1, Episode 8, "The Hobo Code").

Pete's contemptuous attitude also reveals his deep-seated and malignant envy toward Peggy, whose youth, ambition, and talent threaten his progression at the agency. According to Melanie Klein, author of the brief but seminal psychological treatise *Envy and Gratitude*, envy is, by definition, destructive in nature: it "implies robbing the object of what it possesses, and spoiling it."[7] You not only want what the other has, you want to destroy his or her happiness as part of the bargain.

Klein's writings on envy were not about the advertising industry—far from it. She was describing her theories of the infant's psychological experience of feeding. As they eat from the bottle or breast, babies imagine, in a crude, preverbal way, that they own the breast and can control it. So, the mother (or father) who has the milk the baby so desperately wants becomes the object of the infant's envy. It is *as if* the infant thinks: "You have it, I want it, and so I envy you, and want to take it from you. I want to control you—sometimes to such a fever pitch, that it feels to me as if I want to aggressively devour and destroy you."

Though babies are certainly not capable of complex thoughts such as "I envy and want to devour you," they do experience overwhelming jumbles of emotion, according to Klein. Their wanting, coveting, and wanting to control and even destroy are psychological manifestations of their natural needs, instincts, and urges. Adults, like babies, routinely feel intense emotions such as envy of the type described by Klein. And adults who become aware of feelings like this are often uncomfortable.

Exactly what does this have to do with Pete and his critical reaction to Peggy? We know he has slept with her twice: first on the eve of his wedding and again one morning when they both arrived early for work. Their attraction is overpowering—Pete cannot stop himself from being with her on these occasions. The way he deals with feelings that he cannot stem, or understand, is to try to ignore them in the hopes of pushing them away. So, Pete ignores Peggy. He doesn't read her advertising copy, and he doesn't look her way when he walks down the hall to his office. He pretends she does not exist.

Pete's out of sight, out of mind strategy toward Peggy seems to work for a time—until the point when he can no longer employ it. Don tells him Peggy is going to write copy for his new account, Clearasil. Pete is competitive and does not want to be upstaged by any coworker, let alone a woman, but his reactions go deeper than that. Pete envies Peggy's sexuality in the way Klein describes—he wants to possess her body. But he is married, and Peggy is his coworker. So Pete feels overwhelmed by a powerful wish to psychologically destroy that which he so intensely desires but cannot have.

This is what is going on when Pete dismisses and criticizes Peggy for her seductive dancing. He cuts her down because he wants her so badly. Later, he resists her assignment to his team because he wants to thwart her and ruin her success. Pete also seems to want to kill Peggy off psychologically. People who are angry, envious, or threatened may unknowingly seek ways to get rid of the person whose presence they cannot tolerate. Wanting someone off the radar and out of the picture is representative of the psychological (not literal) wish to be rid of or kill them.

But the mind does not work that way—ignoring Peggy certainly doesn't allow Pete to forget about or stop wanting her. Even though he doesn't look Peggy's way when he walks into the office in the morning, he still has her on his mind. After they are intimate for the second time, he tells her, "I'll be honest, [I've thought of you] a few times" (Season 1, Episode 6, "Babylon").

Pete behaves in similar sexist fashion toward his neighbor's young and pretty German au pair, Gudrun. He seduces the unsuspecting girl, basically forcing her to have sex with him—then pretends it never happened (Season 3, Episode 8, "Souvenir"), proving again Pete's tendency to devalue and behave aggressively toward women by treating them as objects for his pleasure and enjoyment. It is only through his growing closeness with Trudy, and his realization that his selfish and insensitive actions do have an impact, that Pete develops empathy and begins to be less governed by his envy.

Pete begins maturing when he recognizes the existence of another being; that Trudy is not just an extension of him. Together they begin to do things less by the book—they skip Roger's daughter's wedding, and he tells her he doesn't want her summering with her family without him anymore, even though all of the rich young wives of the upper crust go away for that season.

While the workplace is different than it was in the middle 1960s—women don't have to work as secretaries, typists, nurses, and stewardesses, and they have a host of opportunities open to them—discrimination persists, but in more subtle forms. The Equal

Rights Amendment did not pass; there is no legislative mandate that women be treated equally. Though conditions have improved, men continue to come out ahead in the workplace, attaining higher positions in corporate America, dominating certain fields like finance, and earning more generous wages for the same jobs.

6

Family and Child Rearing

Don and Betty don't spend all weekend racing from soccer practice to baseball field to piano recital. They aren't preoccupied with Bobby's and Sally's schedules and interests, or focused on their achievements. No one seems to notice that Sally is in considerable emotional pain until she flips: running away to New York City, cutting off her long hair, and fondling herself at a sleepover.

Like the men of his time, Don focuses on work. He loves his children, but they are not on his radar. He certainly never changed a diaper or took on any caregiving duties. And while Betty is around the kids—physically, at least—she doesn't seem to really focus on or interact with them. She is hardly preoccupied with their needs or desires, unlike some mothers today whose own emotional needs leave them with limited distance, physical or psychological, from their children.

Mostly, the Drapers coexist with Sally and Bobby, and don't seem to regard them as separate individuals with their own wants and feelings. Once they have provided food and shelter, they consider the daily work of child care and parenting to be complete.

Fifty years ago, kids often amused themselves by playing with toys, reading books and watching TV, or running around with neighboring kids. If domestic life revolved around anyone, it was the parents. There was no overscheduling of children and no micromanaging of their days. Helicopter mommies had not yet begun to hover—that type of parenting would not surface for years to come. Back then if the children were too young to stay home alone, they went along while their parents accomplished what they wanted or needed to do: grocery shopping, a trip to the beauty salon, social gatherings with adult friends, and perhaps activities Dad might have liked, like ball games or fishing trips.

PARENTING CULTURE

Many women today pursue their personal ambitions through their children. They live vicariously and bolster their own self-esteem through them. Betty Draper could only aspire to goals attained through her husband, though, and did not take pride in her children's efforts and achievements. Sally and Bobby seem to give her no pleasure, and to be of no use to her in this way. If anxiety causes the parents of today to hover and convinces them that days packed with practices and lessons will provide a leg up in the rat races their children will experience in the future, it is a uniquely modern behavior, and Betty would be unable to fathom this. The competitive attitude of millennial parents who treat child rearing as a contact sport would be foreign to her.

Betty's lack of interest in living vicariously through her children's achievements represents one aspect of a larger problem: the inability to know or realize any sort of personal ambition, even a hint of which would have seemed to be unfeminine. This type of prohibition was common among women of the *Mad Men* era, and led to discontentment and disaffection for many—but especially Betty. Unable to know all aspects of her psychology and all parts of herself, she suffers emotionally. For example, thwarted in her desire to model, ashamed at the loss of the gig, and unable to build an identity except as "Mrs. Draper" or "Mommy," she becomes disappointed. She cannot achieve success on her own and cannot pursue other opportunities—what kind of wife would that make her!—so she unconsciously bats these wishes away. Her personal ambition immediately and automatically goes underground. After pushing her dreams and aspirations aside, she is left with only free-floating anxiety, a sense of depression and apathy and confusion.

Betty's mothering, more destructive than either the post-Freudian permissive or the adherence-to-doctrine style, is even worse than what Christopher Lasch decried in his book *The Culture of Narcissism*.[1] And it is deficient by any standards. She lacks emotional availability, and does not really try to understand or support her children; their needs are an annoyance and an inconvenience to her. If healthy or secure attachment develops when a responsive and tuned-in caregiver attends to a child's needs repeatedly over time while also setting appropriate limits, Betty does none of this. She is cold and critical of her children, and ignores their emotional needs and their signals for attention. Sally gets a slap when she cuts her own hair, and her mother excoriates her when she learns her daughter has masturbated at a sleepover. Betty is more worried about her social standing and image than about the cause of Sally's behavior or the feelings that underlie it: loneliness, feelings of being misunderstood, sadness at missing her father, anger at the divorce, and growing up without a suitable model of femininity. All Betty ever seems to say to her daughter is "Go to your room." She does not consider any of the emotions that motivate her children's behaviors or actions—even when Sally is scared of the dark, she does not see that she is in any difficulty. In fact, as we already know, she doesn't seem to notice her children, or concern herself with their wants and needs very much, if at all. At best they are invisible to her, at worst a nuisance. As Betty did not receive the necessary emotional support and nurturance during her childhood, she is unable to give her children what they need emotionally. She has almost no capacity to connect with either of her children.

BETTY AS A WIRE MONKEY

While Betty's situation as a lonely housewife is poignant, it is her style of parenting, which by today's standards is not really parenting at all, that has captured the interest of so many fans of the show. Psychologists have a name for a mother like Betty who does not nurture and has little to give emotionally to her children: to the professionals she is a "wire monkey."

In the 1950s a researcher at the University of Wisconsin named Harry Harlow wondered about the causes, components, and mechanisms of maternal love. In 1957 he took eight neonatal rhesus monkeys (chosen because they show a range of human-like emotions) and paired them with synthetic mommies. Some of the baby monkeys were fed milk by "mothers" made of cold, hard wire; others by "mothers" made of wire but covered in warm, soft terry cloth. Harlow's findings were fascinating: all the babies ate and grew, and all chose to cuddle with the cloth "mother"—regardless of whether they had been fed by the wire ones.

In a related experiment, when a teddy bear beating a scary loud drum was introduced, only those babies who had access to cloth mothers fared well. Though startled, they were not overcome with anxiety. By contrast, those who had no mother figure or wire mommies felt overwhelmed and agitated and threw themselves on the floor, screaming (much like Sally did when Don told her she couldn't live with him). The monkeys without mommies or with wire ones showed their terror and agony in the stressful situation by loudly vocalizing their fear, crouching, rocking back and forth, and sucking. They also had difficulties socializing with peers.

Harlow's findings were educative about the importance of loving maternal figures and caretakers in early childhood. From his monkey studies he concluded that babies needed to form attachments with parental figures in the first months of life. "Contact comfort" was crucial; those deprived of love and "succor" would find it difficult to compensate—even if love was offered at a later point in time.[2]

The rhesus monkeys Harlow studied who had wire mothers demonstrated attachment patterns that were, in a word, insecure. If an infant doesn't have a nurturing caregiver who is responsive to his needs on a regular basis, his future relationships will be characterized by mistrust, insecurity, and possibly a lack of closeness or intimacy with others. Harlow generalized his results to human beings and concluded that—just as psychoanalysts had claimed for decades—solid early attachments and responsive caregivers are necessary in order for individuals to thrive as healthy adults.[3]

According to psychoanalysts and researchers in the field of attachment, Betty's behavior makes her an unresponsive, insensitive, and rejecting "wire mother." She doesn't spend much time with her children, and when she does, she behaves in a critical and cold fashion. On one occasion, Bobby wants attention after Baby Gene's birth and Betty tells him, "Go bang your head against the wall" (Season 3, Episode 6, "Guy Walks into an Advertising Agency"). In today's overly involved zeitgeist it is hard to fathom such laissez-faire parenting.

To some extent, Betty's style of parenting is consistent with social norms (many boomers grew up watching violence on TV until studies revealed such children were plagued with more anxiety and depression than children who did not watch such images), but some of it is likely a repetition of her early years with her parents. Her father, Gene, does try to show kindness to Sally in the months before he dies, even as he and Betty are not very closely connected, despite his attempts at bridging their distance. Gene tries to communicate with Betty, but she cannot engage with him in a meaningful way. He tries to discuss the future with her; what will happen after he is gone. She tells him he is making her feel bad, and that she's still his "little girl." It is as if she implores, "I am still a child. I cannot handle anything difficult." After this exchange, Gene very deliberately tells Sally, "You could really do something—don't let your mother tell you otherwise" (Season 3, Episode 4, "The Arrangements"). His intense focus and investment in Sally seem like an effort to make up for past mistakes raising Betty, such as treating her as incompetent, sheltering her from the real world, and perhaps even focusing more on her brother. He has treated Betty as a house cat, a protected pet not fit to survive in the great wide world. Having seen the results, he wants more for Sally and Bobby.

And Betty's mother is just a memory whom she mourns, crying on the shoulder of her mother's maid. But actions speak louder than words, and watching Betty, it is plausible to conclude that—despite her sadness over her mother's death—their relationship was distant and removed. We don't know much; only that her mother had harshly criticized Betty about her weight, and that Gene had revealed that his late wife had been a drafting engineer. It is worth considering that this informed her parenting style; if she felt she had left an interesting career to raise her children, it is likely she resented them for the life she had to give up.

Despite our lack of specific knowledge about the nature of Betty's relationship with her mother, the ghosts of Betty's early emotionally distant relationships are evident in her current treatment of Sally and Bobby. Betty gives her children what she got from her parents, which isn't much. She recalls that her mother always threatened to slap her when she misbehaved—and we know this to be Betty's go-to disciplinary method with her daughter. In other words, we have heard that Betty's mother was cold and punitive with her. And Betty treats Sally in kind. And if the past offered Betty a dearth of individuals from whom to draw emotional comfort, the present is also lacking. She cannot count on much support from Don, making it difficult for her to dig deep and find emotional supplies to give to their children. None have ever been provided.

Betty's mother and father likely left much of the child care to their maid, as Roger Sterling's family did. And indeed, Betty follows in this tradition; she spends less time with her children than Carla, the housekeeper, does. Given her remoteness, critical attitudes, and anger as an adult, one can speculate that Betty's emotional needs were not met by those who took care of her when she was a child.

Betty seems to be kinder to her children when they are young. As they grow, and as she becomes more and more unhappy and unfulfilled, she begins to take out her negative feelings, problems, and misery on her children, especially on her daughter, Sally. Adults commonly repeat what they do not consciously remember; they put past abuses into action in the present as an attempt to master old trauma. Betty does just this when she slaps and criticizes Sally. She re-creates the relationship she had and the feelings she experienced growing up with her mother.

Harlow anticipated the tendency of children to repeat what went on in their families of origin when they become parents themselves. He designed a study to assess the nature of maternal love in the monkeys who had been raised by wire mommies. When these monkeys grew and reproduced he noticed that many of them became "abusive," a term he applied to their tendency to bite and push away their young. In an extreme case, one monkey raised by a wire mother bit off many of her infant's fingers without provocation.[4] It will not be lost on the astute observer that this tragic anecdote mirrors all too closely Betty's threat to cut off Sally's fingers after learning she has masturbated at a neighbor's house!

Harlow introduced therapy monkeys to help socialize the "abusive" adults. Their behaviors did become less aggressive after they had spent time with therapist peers—but they never grew to love their "abused" offspring. Luckily for Sally, Robby, and Baby Gene, they have contact with Don, Megan, and Betty's second husband, Henry.

BACHELOR NUMBER TWO

Betty marries Henry because he can be a father to her as well as to her children, in some ways. In the scene where Don brings home a sheared Sally, Betty is furious, but Henry tells her, "That's what little girls do." He is the parenting expert in the family, and he urges his wife to be less accusatory and critical of her daughter. At times Henry soothes Betty. When he holds her close and strokes her hair after Sally has gone to her room, Henry is more like a father than a spouse; his reassurances, coddling, and affection almost seem paternal. He mirrors and soothes Betty when he empathizes with her disgust for Don: "You don't think I feel that? . . . My weekends with Ellie were sacrosanct" (Season 4, Episode 5, "The Chrysanthemum and the Sword"). His advice on child rearing (which Betty is inclined to follow) is also educative; he teaches her how to deal with her children—even if she seems unable to absorb his lessons about patience, understanding, and kindness. It is he who urges Betty to seek treatment for Sally when her struggles intensify.

According to Dr. Wednesday Martin, a cultural anthropologist and the author of *Stepmonster*, stepparents (generally mothers, but fathers too) share a common fantasy that they can repair the damage done by divorce and that they can heal fractured families.[5] Despite Henry's attempts at making peace in his new family—we even see him gather his mother and grown daughter, and Betty and her kids, on Thanksgiving—as time goes on, Betty appears to become more and more removed from her children and act in increasingly harsh ways toward them. This begins following the deaths of her mother and father, both of which occur close in time, and continues to spiral after her divorce from Don. Betty slaps Sally, speaks to her in a most critical tone, and makes absolutely no effort to understand her.

One of Betty's parenting lows, psychologically at least, occurs when the mother of one of Sally's friends brings Sally home because she was touching herself at the sleepover. Betty becomes apoplectic. Borrowing from the Code of Hammurabi, she harshly threatens to cut Sally's fingers off to punish Sally for masturbating in public and lying about it. This exchange reveals much about Betty's parenting and about the newly formed Francis family. Betty worries that the neighbor will talk about them, and that everyone will know what Sally did and will view Betty and the Francises with disdain. She is embarrassed and humiliated and takes her fury out on Sally instead of trying to understand and help her. She worries that Sally's actions reflect poorly on her. But Sally's actions are a communication to her mother—she needs assistance to understand her complex and intense feelings. Betty's slapping and ignoring her daughter do not address the underlying difficulties that have caused Sally to cut her hair or the reasons she has touched herself. Sally is angry, confused, and lonely after her parents' divorce. She is also developing into an adolescent and experiencing changes in her body. Fondling herself in a semipublic space represents a communication to her mother that she needs assistance dealing with her feelings.

Betty's form of parenting is detached, critical, and lacking in empathy. Her daughter's needs and feelings do not enter into the equation—especially when Betty herself feels angry, hurt, or embarrassed. She does not view Sally's behaviors as a cry for help or a communication from child to parent. Instead, she just sees Sally as a difficult and bad child. Her main concern seems to be that the neighbors will talk. She is too limited to see that Sally is desperate for help with her feelings.

On several occasions Betty excoriates her daughter for her sexual urges and curiosity—the same qualities she loathes in herself. Betty, too has masturbated (on the fainting couch in her living room, and in her laundry room, leaning on the vibrating washing machine). She cannot tolerate that she had the impulse to touch herself, that she has bodily needs and sensations. She must experience such impulses and their accompanying thoughts and feelings as existing outside of herself because they threaten her sense of emotional equilibrium.

So, Betty behaves in an angry and critical manner toward Sally after her daughter has been caught masturbating. Psychologically, though, what Betty has done is externalize or cast off a part of herself that she feels is shameful and bad, only to see it as belonging to someone else. In effect, she gets rid of the bad, and simultaneously blames another (Sally) for it. Fragile Betty is in effect saying: "I am not the one in the wrong—the bad is outside of me and in Sally." Betty's need for Sally to contain the feelings and behaviors she views as bad and shameful is one way that her psychological fragility makes it difficult for her to parent.

Were Betty more able to deal with her own sexual impulses and fantasies about other men and her own desires for sexual satisfaction, and were she less ashamed of her decision to masturbate, she might have tried to understand Sally's confusion and physical impulses—and she might not have attacked Sally for them. Simply put: Betty hates in Sally what she sees in herself. When Betty meets Dr. Edna, the child analyst she consults about her daughter's masturbation, she tells her, "I feel like Sally did this to punish me" (Season 4, Episode 5, "The Chrysanthemum and the Sword").

Sally's masturbation episode speaks volumes about Betty's psychological and parenting styles. She protects herself from threatening thoughts and feelings, and from myriad situations that make her feel powerless, defective, and unhappy, by unconsciously shifting her perception. In a split second she gets rid of the bad and turns it around so that she does not own it. For example: Sally is the problem, Don is the problem. Betty is not. She views her ex-husband and her daughter without nuance.

By comparison, Betty seems to put Henry on a pedestal and idealize him. He is worldly and has more life experience. He has raised a family and has navigated relationships with his now adult daughter, and he has held a job in the outside world—all things Betty has not. He communicates with her and is kind to her in a way Don could never be. And he is a man, so he must know what is best for their family. This is Betty in her relationships. Like she did with Don, Betty takes Henry's advice and listens to him almost without reserve. She views Henry in the other extreme—he is all good. Betty does not seem to relate to anyone in an equal or mutual way. This contributes to her feelings of loneliness, as she does not really know all aspects, good and bad, of those around her.

At one point her loneliness leads her to befriend Glen, a neighbor's child. They hold hands in a rather odd manner. Betty doesn't have a sense of how to properly negotiate the boundaries in her relationships. When things don't go her way she pouts or gets angry. She often needs soothing and attention herself. Feeling lonely, empty, and deprived emotionally, she often fails to give her children the care and attention they require. Ironically, she becomes physically affectionate with Glen—though they do no more than hold hands and silently sit together. Though they just console each other, Betty's loneliness has caused her to cross a line. She seeks love and companionship, and she uses Glen, a child, to provide comfort, instead of forming friendships with people her own age.

So, given Betty's limitations, it is no surprise that Sally is unhappy and seems to struggle. Her father has left. She and her brothers were not given much of an explanation. And her mother is usually angry, critical, or just plain cold to her. Sally's actions, such as running away to Don's, cutting her hair, and touching herself at a friend's house, all can be understood to be communications by her to the adults in her life. Sally is bright and perceptive, and she knows the adults are up to more than they let on. She cannot rely on them to calm her doubts or answer her questions. So, Sally puts feelings and her internal life into action because her emotions and thoughts are too overwhelming to manage.

Acting on feelings without knowing your own motivations is quite common—and internal life is complicated for anyone, especially a precocious ten-year-old. Sally is likely coping with feelings of loss, sadness, abandonment, loneliness, as well as rivalry with her younger brothers, and feelings about her prepubescent body and about growing up. Feeling out of control and in order to deal with the onslaught of everything she is experiencing, Sally takes the Metro-North train to New York City.

None of the adults ever really talks to Sally because they do not focus on her or know how to read a child. Don isn't big on feelings, and Betty needs a parent just as much as her daughter does; this is magnified after she loses her mother and father. At Henry's insistence, she does find a child psychoanalyst for Sally—and she seems to benefit from talking to Dr. Edna just as much as her daughter does.

Don is warmer and more caring than Betty. At times he seems able to trust his instincts as a parent. Parenting can't be easy for Don. With little more than good intentions and instincts to guide him, Don tries to support his children. But at times he falters, even as he is sincere. In all of his close relationships he is ambivalent; he gives mixed signals and struggles to retain emotional intimacy.

LONGING FOR LOVE

Mary Ainsworth, a developmental psychologist who studied attachment patterns in young children, designed a study in the 1970s in which the behavior of twelve-month-olds was observed during interactions with their caregivers and in new situations. As the children played in an unfamiliar room, a stranger entered, and after a few minutes their mothers quietly left. The mothers returned after a few minutes to their typically upset children. The babies displayed three distinct patterns in their interactions with their caregivers. *Securely attached* babies related well and warmly to the mothers, made eye contact with them, and felt safe in their presence. They were initially afraid of the stranger and ran to hug their mothers, but eventually felt comfortable in exploring the environment with occasional glances at their mothers for assurance. Babies in the second, or *ambivalently attached*, group exhibited intense emotion much of the time, such as squalling and crying, and related to their mothers in a way that was a mixed bag emotionally; they first clung to, then rejected their mothers. They vacillated between very needful fits and behaviors that were ignoring, such as looking away or creating physical distance between themselves and their mothers. The third group were *avoidantly attached.* They did not seem attached and did not get close to their mothers, emotionally or physically.[6] Avoidant babies ignored the return of their mothers, didn't count on them for support, and used an indifferent, self-contained posture to protect themselves in a stressful stranger situation. Ainsworth saw avoidant children as suffering from emotional pain and difficulties, and posited that they had experienced painful separations. She concluded: "The [ambivalent] baby fears he will not get enough of what he wants. The [avoidant] baby fears what he wants."[7]

Don's distancing behavior, lack of empathy, and tendency to push others away place him within the third group, those showing *avoidant attachment styles.* In the language of attachment theorists, Don is overly self-reliant, defiant, and detached. He cannot trust others sufficiently to form close relationships. His avoidant style does not come as a surprise, as he never had the opportunity to form a close and loving relationship with his mother, who died when he was an infant, or with his alcoholic father, who worked day and night, leaving Don with a critical and cold stepmother. From a history of loss and a rejecting stepmother, he learned early on not to count on or trust the people around him.

But beneath his callous behaviors and avoidant style, Don continues to long for his mother's love and for the father he lost. He plays out his longings, albeit in a paradoxical fashion, by seducing and then abandoning or being abandoned by a series of beautiful and exciting women (Rachel, Betty, Faye)—if he unconsciously provokes others to reject him, or if he rejects them, he feels more in control of the demise of the relationship, thus bringing about the expected outcome and mastering his anxiety about loss.

Attachment theory explains much in terms of how adults like Don relate to one another, but it does not explain how their overall personality or character is formed in adult life. In terms of that, Don can, as we already know, be understood as someone who suffers from narcissistic vulnerability, or deficits in self-esteem that affect his overall personality and interfere with his day-to-day emotional regulation and functioning. His history of early loss and deprivation accounts for his considerable fragility and explains a great deal about the reasons for his wounded self-esteem.

Don suffers from a deep wound that makes him seek constant validation and reinforcement from those around him. Just as Don fears the feelings and needs deep inside of him, he is frightened of those who try to get close, and feels terrified they will try to dominate him. Control is a big issue for Don, because as a child he had none. He lost his mother and later his father, his stepmother treated him harshly and favored his half brother, all very difficult and painful circumstances. Someone who experiences trauma in early life comes to be filled with persistent anxiety, which he or she unwittingly attempts to stem by controlling the present environment. This means that Don and only Don decides when and if to let anyone in—and he revokes his love abruptly whenever it suits him.

Like many who suffer from narcissistic vulnerability, Don cannot bear to look inward; it is too depressing. So he denies his feelings and runs from them because it is the only way he can survive psychologically. Should he fail to ward off the anxiety and despair he feels, his emotional well-being will be rocked. After Don's "lost weekend," drinking heavily with at least two different women, including an unfamiliar waitress, he puts on a brave face and insists that all is well. But he soon crumbles when Anna, "the only person in the world who really knew [him]" dies (Season 4, Episode 7, "The Suitcase"). Don waits too long to return Anna's niece Stephanie's telephone call because he cannot face hearing the news of Anna's death. He misses the chance to pay her a final visit, though she is someone he holds dear. And of course, he drinks heavily to avoid his pain.

This is Don in relationships—he is terrified, and regularly runs from intimate involvements, even those he has initiated. He routinely displays a general lack of empathy for those who try to get close, including his ex-wife, partners, and coworkers. His lack of empathy is not just selfish insensitivity, though; it is driven by his need to close off the frightened child within, and represents an attempt to shore up a brittle, fragile self that he fears could cave in at any moment.

Betty; his daughter, Sally; his office romance Faye; and his new fiancée, Megan, are all connected to Don at different points in time, and his on-again, off-again relationships with them reflect his difficulties connecting in relationships. He can be loving and sensitive, callous and unempathetic, or cold and guarded, depending on the day and even the minute. This plasticity makes him difficult to read, and causes his relationships to suffer. With Betty, Don remains opaque, secretive, and closed off to her needs. With Faye, he vacillates between loving her and using her, then cheats on her at the first opportunity with Megan (Season 4, Episode 11, "Chinese Wall").

In proposing to Megan, Don is also serving his own needs. When he tells the American Cancer Society about writing his op-ed piece, "It was an impulse, because I knew what I needed to do to move forward" (Season 4, Episode 13, "Tomorrowland"), Don might as well have been talking about proposing to Megan. Right after psychologist Faye encourages him to "resolve the past" that continues to haunt him, Don impulsively and instinctively chooses not to do so. He invites Megan to California to babysit for his children while he works, and quickly proposes to her because her beauty and her easy interactions with Sally, Bobby, and Gene, in sharp contrast to Betty's rigid ways, win him over. Proposing to Megan is Don's attempt at survival.

TROPHY WIFE, TROPHY LIFE

Don marries Betty because she is a beautiful trophy. She is from the Main Line in Philadelphia, has graduated from a prestigious "Seven Sister," a private college for women, and exudes wealth and class. He, by contrast, is a farmer's son who quit night school to sell furs. Don woos and wins the young model, and takes a step up in the world. Once he makes the leap to Roger Sterling's firm, he focuses on establishing himself there, and obviously succeeds with aplomb.

Don's focus is on himself. His attention and worries do not include his wife. He is constantly internally preoccupied, and nothing else exists when he wants something. We see this clearly in Season 4 when he seduces and casts aside a much younger secretary (Episode 2, "Christmas Comes but Once a Year") and begins a passionate affair with the research psychologist, Faye. With Faye, the entire relationship occurs on Don's terms. She even compromises her business ethics for Don, breaking a confidence to another client that is unhappy with its ad agency, and arranging a pitch meeting for Don—even though at that very moment Don is cheating on her with his newest secretary and soon-to-be fiancée, Megan (Season 4, Episode 11, "Chinese Wall").

Don's relationships are erratic and, at times, distant because feelings and emotional intimacy frighten him—and he routinely avoids that which threatens his self-esteem. His denial occurs largely on an unconscious level, and his lack of insight into his emotions causes him to act out his fears. That which is avoided comes back unexpectedly to haunt him, however.

If Don's running from the past, and the impact these actions have on his family members (including Betty and his half brother, Adam), are confusing to the viewer, his relationships outside the family are equally confounding. Don and Peggy share a special bond at work; he turns to her when he has no one else, but he derides and chastises her any time there is a problem with the work produced by any member of the creative team. Peggy has earned Don's respect, yet his approval is fleeting, and she must continually jump through hoops. He is kind and mentoring one moment, cruel the next. After months of critical attacks on her work, he unexpectedly leans on her for support when he is desperate and alone in the middle of the night (Season 4, Episode 7, "The Suitcase").

Don's behavior toward Peggy, kind and cutting by turns, mirrors the way he treats women with whom he is romantically involved. While he seems to blow hot and cold, his behaviors are a function of his narcissism and fragile self. Though Don appears to be strong and successful, he is vulnerable at the core. His self-image turns on his latest failure or success, and he needs the constant shoring up of those around him. He seeks out external sources—beautiful women, high-end restaurants, a lovely home and fancy car, a Clio award—to boost his ego, but these efforts bring only temporary satisfaction. And the cycle of damaged, brittle self-esteem and external bolstering continues.

Don views himself as a hypocrite who says one thing and portrays himself a certain way, but then takes another, more self-serving path. When Don looks in the mirror when high and has a flashback to the hobo and his hypocritical father and stepmother, he sees parallels in his own life, and does not like what he sees. He knows that his lies and actions hurt people. And at times of clarity, he hates himself for his hypocrisy and his cruel and hostile turns.

Don never got to know his biological mother, a prostitute who died in childbirth. Growing up, he did not get much in the way of love or warmth from his father or stepmother. Don seems to find a mother in Anna Draper, though. She alone knows that he has stolen her husband's identity and has deserted the army, and she loves and accepts him despite these misdeeds. Anna's love for Don is unconditional, unwavering. In these ways her feelings for Don resemble a mother's love for her child.

Don is caring toward Anna too. He pays her mortgage and becomes distraught when he hears of her illness—so much so that he falls apart when her niece calls to notify him that Anna has died. He cannot will himself to pick up the phone and he goes on a drinking bender to avoid dealing with the reality of the situation. While Don loves Anna, he is limited in his ability to be emotionally present at the time of a crisis.

But while Don falls short in his ability to be there at the time of Anna's death, and seems to lack empathy for Betty, he usually manages to respond to the emotional needs of his children—though he is far from being always present, consistent, and reliable. As a parent, he gives more than he got—he does the best that he can, and it appears that his efforts are often enough to meet his children's needs for love and support.

Don tries to be there for his children, and wants to be available for them. Still, he runs out of Sally's birthday party, leaving Betty to host alone—in front of the whole neighborhood. What drives Don to run off and disappear from Sally's party? Don is someone who acts quickly whenever he has an unpleasant feeling, and seeks to get rid of it. When his neighbor talks about "having it all," Don appears to feel discontented, hemmed in—and he feels trapped. He has deceived others, hidden his identity, and feels he has been a fraud. The more he hides and the more hypocritical his actions, the more isolated and distant from others he feels. No one really knows the true Don. While he has a wife and a family, he is not truly close to any of them. He keeps secrets and maintains his distance, especially from Betty. Their picture-perfect marriage and family is empty and depressing. When his neighbors gather and he sees how insular their community is, how everyone gossips, and how the divorced Helen Bishop is cast out, it feels as though life offers only two extremes: suffocate in the suburbs, where you are forced to be exactly like everyone else, or be an outcast. Don does not like either path, and feels he has no good options—he does not want to live life as a single man; he sees how Helen is treated like a pariah. Yet his is not the life he envisions for himself, and he does not feel like part of his rigid and confining community.

When his neighbor comments on Don's "perfect" family and home, Don appears to panic. He runs. He might be fleeing his own feelings of need and dependency. He also might feel anxious that his neighbor's comment raised unknown intense emotions—Don absolutely does not like what he does not understand or control as it makes him feel defective and broken. He has created the image of a family that he's seen in Coca-Cola ads and on television shows, and it's empty at heart.

Those who feel broken act in a compensatory fashion to fight off their fragility and perceived defects. When Don is faced with a feeling or a situation he cannot handle, it makes him feel anxious and inadequate. He does not want to feel this way—it is too threatening to his ego. It is plausible that he flees in order to protect himself and get away from that which makes him feel fragile. He does not try to understand what is going on inside with his emotional state.

Don's actions embarrass Betty, though the children are too young to know what is going on. He appears to be totally lacking in empathy toward her. Being entirely unable to discern what might hurt another human being can occur in those who, like Don, have experienced profound early losses. Don has never been admired or seen the shine of love in the eyes of a caring mother. Such gaps in childhood nurturance bring wounds that cut deep. Don's self-esteem is permanently scarred.

This also explains at least part of the reason why Don cheats on Betty. If empathy refers to the ability to be sensitive to, understand, or vicariously experience the feelings and thoughts of another individual, Don fails to do this whenever Betty's interests do not coincide with his. While empathic people can often anticipate the needs of those around them, Don thinks mostly about himself. When he needs to flee or seek the comfort of another woman to escape the complex and disturbing emotions that plague him, thoughts of Betty and the kids take a backseat.

When Don is with a lover, Betty and any awareness of conflict or unpleasant feelings are removed from his consciousness. They are closed off, shoved back, pushed into the recesses of the mind, much like the physical action Don takes of locking photographs of his parents and dead brother in the box in his desk.

Don is prone to action and is frightened of feeling too deeply. So he tries to immediately get rid of that which feels too threatening by performing some action that he hopes will fix the situation and help him to manage his feelings. Don consciously and intentionally pushes things to the corners of his mind in an action called "repudiation." He knows he has stolen an identity—he just doesn't think about it most of the time. When he is having sex with someone else, he just doesn't think about Betty.

Don disavows the existence of his brother. When he locks photographs of his past away in a drawer, Don hopes that if he shoves them, and the accompanying emotion or situation, out of sight, he will succeed in conquering them mentally. Though his reality testing is completely intact, he pushes away some of the contents of his mind, at least for the time being. He prefers not to remember he is Dick Whitman, and that he has a family, including an adoring younger half brother, that he has left behind. He distances himself from the truth, though he remains aware of it.

EMPATHY AND PARENTING

Parental love takes many forms: affection, cuddling, teasing, playing, and feeding. It is also often revealed in the form of empathy for one's children. Empathy is one of the things that enables parents to nurture and support their children. It refers to the ability to tune in to someone else's feelings or experience—but in such a way as to know that the emotion you pick up on belongs to the other, not to you. It is the psychological equivalent of being able to step into someone's shoes, intuit what they feel, and step back out.

We know that Don lacks empathy for Betty. After her mother dies, her father brings a new girlfriend, Gloria, with him when he visits the Drapers. "My mother just died. He hovers over her just like he used to hover over my mom and they were together for over forty years." "She seems like a nice lady" is all Don can say to his wife, who is clearly grieving her mother and looking for comfort from her husband (Season 1, Episode 10, "Long Weekend").

Because he is unable to empathize with Betty, Don is also unable to intuit that she needs attention, caring, and compassion. It is possible that Betty's grieving reminds him that he never knew his mother, so he cannot tolerate it. He is sensitive to loss and raw at the possibility of reawakening old feelings; it is an Achilles heel for him. But, more likely, Don never got much in the way of compassion and empathy—and as a result, he has none to give, even to his wife, even when she has suffered a major loss.

Curiously, Don does not lack empathy for his children. In a way that is common to the character, Don mistreats Betty by disappearing on her at an important moment, but contiguously in time, shows his daughter better treatment. He runs out during Sally's birthday party, for example. But when he returns, his daughter is excited to see him; they kiss and hug warmly and he brings her a puppy as a gift. Betty feels hurt and abandoned, though. We see Don's ability to mistreat and hurt his wife, while being kind and affectionate to one of his children, time and again. When he does try with Betty, it is by bringing her a gold watch and giving her a pep talk about how she has "everything." But his concern for her does not seem to run as deep as it does for his children.

Psychologists know the tendency to be able to give of oneself to children even when one generally cannot give emotionally to peers or loved ones to be an expression of self-loving and caring. It is quite common to give love to a child—an extension of the self—and in so doing to feel that one is receiving love, caring, compassion, and concern by proxy. When Don is kind and parental to his children, he feels cared for as a by-product. Giving love makes him feel as if he is getting love. He takes comfort and succor in the nurturing. But this happens out of his conscious awareness.

DON AS FATHER, SON, AND BROTHER

Don is fragile, and his vulnerability lies just below his competent and handsome veneer. His fears and insecurities seep out, even as he goes to great lengths and spends lots of time trying to repair his broken, wounded self. He was constantly rejected, ignored, and criticized by his disapproving stepmother. There was no warmth between them. She did not love or want him.

Don ran away as soon as he was old enough to join the army. But the loveless beginnings and deep emotional void stayed with him. He worried that he didn't measure up, and he was sensitive to criticism, easily angered, and desperate to rise above his childhood poverty. He was also alone and lonely. And the loneliness persisted, despite his finding a wife, starting a family, and having many encounters with women along the way.

Eventually, Don decides to attend his son Gene's birthday party even though he is not really invited. He loves Gene and wants him to know that he is his father, not Henry. Don seems to keep the rejecting parts of his psychology out of his interactions with his children.

His half brother, Adam, isn't quite as lucky, though. Don acts very aggressively with him and is partly to blame for Adam's shocking and desperate act of suicide.

We may understand the reasons behind Don's actions even as we might not condone them. But Adam must have been blindsided by Don's cruel, rejecting tone and by the finality of his good-bye. To Adam, Don's behaviors must have seemed hostile and aggressive. Don pushes him away and will not listen to anything he has to say. He does not allow himself to take an interest in his half brother or to desire any closeness with him. Adam tries to give love freely; Don does not want it. Adam tries to get close to Don. Don tells him he is not going to have a relationship with him—this type of rejection is deeply personal in nature.

The interactions with Adam give us valuable insight into Don's unconscious mind. For instance, his treatment of his brother can be explained as a type of visceral rejection of his own feelings and of reality—he disavows what is potentially upsetting to him.

People regularly use Don's "out of sight, out of mind" strategy. In Don's day, unplugging the phone or having the secretary "take a message" served this purpose. Today, technology confers other methods, such as breakup by text message or defriending your ex on Facebook. Such technological advances make avoidance by secretary or answering machine look quaint by comparison.

Out of sight, out of mind does work—but usually only temporarily. In Don's case he is confronted by an actual person from the past. But in most cases it can be less dramatic. Seeing a photo, hearing a song, being asked an innocent question takes our minds back to a place we might not want to go. Individuals hope that pushing things out of awareness will do the trick. And it sometimes does—but not for long.

This is because the mind doesn't work this way, of course. Don can't lock up his thoughts and ignore his feelings forever. Don's flashbacks are the result of emotions and thoughts that he has tried to forget. He pushes them away by distracting himself, self-medicating with alcohol, or physically running away from difficult, upsetting situations. Sometimes his forgetting is intentional; other times it happens automatically and unconsciously. But eventually Don is confronted with what he has tried to forget. Powerful emotions and thoughts will inevitably resurface; getting rid of threatening ideas or feelings by pushing them away or refusing to acknowledge them is not a permanent solution.

Parenting and caring for children is important to Don. He chooses Megan in large part because she is maternal—and rejects Faye partly because she is not. When Faye cannot calm Sally at the office it marks the beginning of the end of their relationship; Don takes his beautiful new secretary, Megan, on his family trip to California so that she can help him with the child care. Her gentle discipline, patience, and French schoolgirl songs charm Don. He proposes. She meets his needs for sex, companionship, and mothering—for him and the children (that is to say, she meets them for now). She is beautiful, polished, maternal, and young, and she represents a possible future, not the past (as the older, more psychological Faye does). So, Faye is out, and Megan gets the engagement ring. On one level, Don has chosen Megan over Faye because he believes Megan will make a good stepmother for his children.

Don is not expected to take parenting leave, to work part-time, or to see his kids more than every other weekend. The attitudes and traditional gender roles espoused by him and Betty were typical of the 1960s. Mostly he focuses on work, and does not rearrange his life according to his kids' schedules. In his view, child care is reserved for the women.

Watching Don and Betty parent, we are confronted with the reality of how difficult it is to overcome certain aspects of our own childhoods. When the going gets tough, the Drapers are all too similar to Harlow's monkeys that had been raised by wire mommies before becoming parents themselves. Though Henry provides soothing for Betty, and Megan provides mothering for Don and his children, it seems unlikely these "present-day" adult spouses will be able to compensate for the harshness and limitations of Don and Betty's childhoods. But if the elder Drapers' emotional futures look somewhat dismal, Sally's is more promising. She regularly sees a child analyst (or at least she has until the Francis clan moves to Rye). Sally's relationship with Dr. Edna and the insights it offers her might enable her to break some of the difficult patterns of engagement that have been passed down by her parents.

7

Sex, Marriage, and the Politics of Infidelity

It was the era of double standards. Men could have premarital sex without ruining their reputations; women who did so were sullied. Men could have extramarital sex without ruining their reputations; women who did so were ruined. Men could father a child out of wedlock without destroying their reputations; women who did so, well . . . we all know where this is going.

We've seen radical cultural shifts in *Mad Men*'s four seasons, but no letup so far in these pervasive double standards between women and men's sexual conduct. The gynecologist who prescribes Peggy the pill tells her not to become the "town pump" in the pilot. In Season 4, when Joan and Roger seek a "rabbit test," the doctor judgmentally accuses Roger of "using" her (Episode 10, "Hands and Knees").

Back then men had all the freedom, all the opportunities. As we already know, women were second-class citizens. Men could engage in endless dalliances or long-standing extramarital relationships and people generally looked the other way. Reputations suffered a black eye, if that, but were generally not destroyed.

Despite this apparent freedom of choice, most men seemed to

prefer marriage—and some even wed more than once. Roger and Mona split only so he could marry the much younger Jane. Henry chooses to marry Betty, despite his mother's assertion that he could just have his way with a woman like her. And Don proposes to Megan, even though he has just gained the right to have multiple affairs without sneaking around on a wife, confirming Faye's prediction that he'd be remarried with a year (Season 4, Episode 2, "Christmas Comes but Once a Year"). Don realizes that he prefers the married life—with a comfortable, maintained home and companionship—to his dark West Village apartment and loneliness. He prefers being idealized in love to wrestling with his true identity.

Women who played around, on the other hand, were viewed with disdain. They were judged to be "that kind of girl." And once a woman earned this reputation, it could permanently bar her from finding a spouse.

Divorced women were another matter altogether. They often felt stigmatized, and were sometimes even shunned. People viewed divorcées as "different." They were even seen as potential husband stealers—as though their mere existence posed a threat to home and hearth and the societal status quo. Many divorced women, like Betty's neighbor Helen, who was whispered about in their homogeneous suburban community, felt isolated and ashamed. But they did not occupy the place at the bottom of the barrel. That lowly position was reserved for the single, unwed mothers.

So for all those keeping score: men five, women zero. Don, Roger, Pete, and the rest could marry, live in comfortable homes with lovely families, and succeed at work. If all this weren't enough, they could also have some fun on the side. And they did. While married to Betty, Don has sustained flings with Rachel, Midge, and Suzanne. And while courting Faye, he dates Bethany and plays around with his secretary, as well as with whatever down-on-her-luck waitress he can manage to charm. Plus, he wooes and proposes to Megan, all behind Faye's back. Likewise, Roger has a years-long affair with Joan before marrying Jane—while married to Mona—and this doesn't discourage him from frolicking with the twin teenagers he picked up at a photo shoot. Pete is no Boy Scout either, cheating on Trudy at least three times, but his antics seem tame by comparison.

Clearly the admen played around with minimal consequences to their jobs and reputations, though Don and Roger do wind up divorced. At Sterling Cooper everyone seems to have sex with everyone, and it all seems to be about power. Peggy sleeps with Pete and doesn't tell him about the resulting baby until she's given it up. She says, "I wanted other things"—perhaps she sought to retain a modicum of power in the only way she could. Harry Crane sleeps with one of the secretaries just to be one of the boys and consolidate his position on the team, even though he loves his wife, and even though his indiscretion makes him feel guilty and miserable. He apparently feels so guilty he confesses, and we see him sleeping in the office for a while. Betty, too, grabs at the little bit of power she can—after Jimmy Barrett throws her husband's affair in her face, she throws Don out. Subsequently Don misuses his position at the office when he sleeps with his eager, admiring secretary, Allison, and casts her aside. Feeling used and humiliated, and with no power to wield, Allison decides to quit. And Joan wields a good deal of sexual power by strutting around and forcing everyone to notice her assets. She enjoys being looked at and takes every opportunity to win each and every man's attention. She also sleeps with several people who work in the office and outside of it—and does not apologize for this. Some women who do not have power in their own right take it by affiliating themselves with men in positions of power. Joan does something like this when she has a long-standing affair with Roger. Perhaps she subscribes to the view that "no one will challenge you if you sleep with the boss." But she also seems to care for him. Either way, being affiliated with a powerful man seems to confer power on Joan; after she quits she is able to get her job back when she needs it, and she does not get fired when times are tough and they have to make cuts.

WORKING GIRLS

In Joan and Peggy's time, only 30 percent of woman with children under the age of five were employed. Currently, 65 percent of mothers with preschoolers and 79 percent of mothers of older children are employed at least part-time outside the home.[1] Back in 1965, woman who never married were called spinsters. It was assumed they could not get a man. But when men were unmarried, it was presumed this was their choice. They were viewed as swingers or fun-loving "bachelors," though they were pitied if they remained single when they got older.

Peggy, like Ms. Blankenship, is single, at least for the moment. Everyone tells her to go out and look for a husband. She prefers to work late. But her story has not yet been determined; if she chooses to continue to put work first, staying late instead of going out to socialize, will she sabotage her chances of finding someone? Women like Peggy who pursued careers over marriage or who waited to marry later in life were unusual in the mid 1960s, though they have become increasingly common today. In 1970 only 28 percent of the adult population was single, for example, but now, 45 percent of adults are not married.[2]

Likewise, there are more never-married single mothers now than ever before. Many have chosen to give birth at an older age than their mothers and grandmothers did.[3] Birth rates for women between the ages of thirty and thirty-four and thirty-five and thirty-nine are up 2 percent; and those for woman between the ages of forty and forty-four have risen 3 percent.

After Peggy and Pete have sex early one morning at the office, over time we see her looking a bit rounder, and the men begin to make fun of her. Joan also makes derogatory comments about Peggy's shape. But Peggy ignores the jokes and jabs of her colleagues. One day she bends over and her skirt tears. So she begins to wear baggy clothing every day. She continues to focus on her job and to nail it. She is apparently myopic in her vision, and immune to the office's insults.

PEGGY'S DENIAL

Peggy carries and delivers a full-term baby—yet she remains convinced she has not been pregnant. What happened to her? Back then less was understood about brain chemistry and psychopathology. What was then called "a mental breakdown" might today be classified as severe postpartum depression. But Peggy's departure from reality seemed to occur long before her postpartum stay on the psych unit. She carried a live baby inside her womb for nine months, and she did not know she was pregnant.

How could Peggy not have noticed a pregnancy? Simply put: denial. Though Peggy is usually quite in control of her mind and emotions, and though she seems to understand herself, her ambitions, and her feelings about her coworkers, she is unable to process the information of her out-of-wedlock pregnancy. She is uneducated about sex and birth control. She does not lose touch with reality overall, but she cannot accept the facts about one particular set of circumstances, so she denies them. This occurs automatically, and not by choice.

Peggy's brain cannot wrap itself around something so painful and unacceptable to her standards of decorum and religion. So she fails to notice the changes in her body, and is oblivious to her burgeoning size and the ceasing of her menses. Even after her contractions have begun, causing her to go to the hospital, and even when the doctor puts her hand on her abdomen, presumably so she can feel the baby kick, her denial remains in place. Despite contractions, a medical opinion, and fetal movement, she tells the doctor that it isn't possible. He immediately calls for a psychiatric consult (Season 1, Episode 13, "The Wheel").

Denial is something the mind uses to protect itself from the prospect of imminent and severe emotional pain. The knowledge that she has had a baby would threaten her idea of who she is (a good Catholic and respectable working woman), so she automatically and unconsciously shuts this information out. A baby would also threaten her ability to achieve success at the office. Peggy could not be a single mother and a copywriter; this simply was not done. So, after her baby is born she attempts to get rid of any loving feelings and guilt in order to preserve the status quo. She cannot completely do this, though, and she winds up in a psychiatric ward, not fully in touch with reality, grieving, and guilty. Her denial serves as a protective shield—it keeps her mind from integrating information that would be too emotionally distressing.

As we have seen in chapter 3, "Working Stiffs," Peggy also needs to viscerally deny a baby because to acknowledge its existence would force her to confront the harsh and all-too-painful reality that she will chose work over an infant—a set of circumstances too shameful and tragic for her to acknowledge. Instead, she just does not let herself know this dilemma exists. In a flashback we learn that even after Peggy has given birth and has been told that she has delivered a baby boy, she continues to struggle mentally. When a doctor comes to her bedside to assess her mental state, she tells him the name of the president and of the hospital—proving she is alert and oriented to time and place. But when he asks why she is in a hospital, Peggy still cannot tell him.

She spends time on the psych ward while her mother and sister cover for her by making up a story that she has tuberculosis. Don visits the ward—which makes her mother and sister suspect he is the baby's father. When he sees Peggy, Don doesn't judge her. He tries to help. He advises her to move forward: "This never happened" (Season 2, Episode 5, "The New Girl").

Denial does not always have to be this dramatic, though. People routinely use it in milder forms. Someone who has been warned by a physician that eating high-cholesterol foods will lead to a heart attack but continues to do so is also using a milder form of denial. Such people often think, "It won't happen to me." Cigarette smokers also think and behave in this way.

As we've seen, Joan and Peggy generally manage to make their way through life and to mostly bring about their desired outcomes, whether at work or personally. Don, on the other hand, seems to struggle. Sure, he makes a splash on Madison Avenue and earns a lot of money, but in many ways he defeats his own conscious aims. His problems with anger are a big reason behind his largely self-defeating tendencies.

ANGER MANAGEMENT 101

Don has difficulty managing his emotions, so he acts out in aggressive and controlling ways in order to feel more powerful and in command. His frailties and aggressive maneuvers are characteristic of someone who has had a history of parental loss and a chaotic early childhood.

Those who have experienced early trauma such as frequent separations, or loss of a parent (due to death or illness, for example)—and Don has been through all of the above, losing not one parent, but both—never really get over their pain. As adults they constantly seek to bind their anxiety and salve their wounds.

Many attempt to hide from vulnerable feelings by seeking out external sources of bolstering. In Don's case these include beautiful women to admire him, alcohol to numb him, dinners out in fancy restaurants, client praise, and rooms in posh hotels so he can feel shored up and important, instead of damaged and afraid.

Those, like Don, who had inconsistent or rejecting early caregivers also often develop fragile self-esteem and feel undeserving—they fear losing those they love in the present, and they believe they deserve very little in life. Don's particular brand of fragility is to feel he deserves punishment. This leads him to provoke others to anger and to induce them to abandon him.

Why does Don feel he deserves punishment? He endured years of neglect and verbal abuse by his stepmother. Her harsh criticism and attacking words have become part of him; he has internalized them to the point where her overly critical attitude has become his. He feels he does not measure up, and deep down he believes he deserves to suffer. So, he inflicts pain on himself by unconsciously playing out his history of loss in adulthood. First he loses Rachel, then Betty. Provoking others to leave him is Don's way of repeating the trauma he endured at a young age when he was left by his mother.

Don does not allow himself to get close and be vulnerable most of the time. He seeks to control most aspects of the relationship he has with all of the women who fall for him. Don is so self-preoccupied and closed off from the experience of others, and is so terrified of being abandoned, that he cannot understand that his lovers exist outside of him and his wants and his needs. To see them as separate would require acknowledging the impermanence of the relationship. Once he acknowledges that someone is separate, he realizes that he cannot control them and could lose them. So, Don tries to control every interaction as a way to deny that others exist outside of and apart from him—and as a way to avoid confronting the painful potential of loss. His pattern of regulating the pace of relationships and exercising control over others feels aggressive to the women with whom Don enters into relationships.

Why is aggression so common for Don? And why does he need to control everyone in his orbit? Faye would view this as being all about his childhood (Season 1, Espisode 2, "Christmas Comes but Once a Year"). Don did not have parents who could help him make sense of emotions—there was no one to help him metabolize, label, or understand frightening and intense feelings, and no one to teach him how to soothe himself, so his feelings have become overpowering and unmanageable. And when anger is felt at this level of intensity it can become so terrifying that it feels as though it will destroy the individual, or cause him to lose his mind.

Anger of this scale becomes so difficult to tolerate that many seek to get rid of it, and can unwittingly act it out in their relationships. For example, someone like Don might not experience himself as hostile, but might act in ways that provoke others. They may become angry and fight with him, but he does not feel responsible or accept his role in the argument. He might not know he is angry but might see the anger as coming from outside of him. For example, though he has had a series of extramarital affairs, he is not aware of any of his own bad feelings about his marriage or home life. When Betty finds out about one of the women he has been with, Don's only experience of the situation is that Betty is the angry one. When she confronts him and refuses to sleep in their bed, Don feels that she is causing an argument; she is too emotional, and she is rocking the boat. He is unaware of his own hostility toward his wife, his feeling hemmed in by her, or his unresponsiveness to her. Likewise, when Roger confronts Don following the flirtations of a drunken Jane, Don tells him, "No one thinks you're happy. They think you're foolish."

As he does with Betty, Don experiences all the bad feelings as coming from Roger. Don does not want to discuss intimate feelings with him, does not like to be bound to or to answer to anyone, and he is furious at him for marrying Jane; she was Don's secretary and knew all of his secrets. Roger's decision to cross this boundary makes Don feel violated and enraged. Don is mostly unaware of his own anger and does not understand that his behaviors have been provocative, however. He feels their disagreement is all Roger's fault.

In addition to provoking people to deal with his overwhelming levels of anger, Don seeks out troubled relationships that mirror those he had in the past with his emotionally unavailable early caregivers. For Don and others like him, aggressive actions and caring ones, as well as anger and love, become fused. He repeats a pattern of engaging in troubled relationships because he views love and hostility, or even love and violence, to be connected. For Don and others, love is equated with pain and suffering.

Take Suzanne Farrell. Don's affair with Suzanne, Sally's teacher, can also be seen as a manifestation of his self-defeating tendencies. She has met Betty. She sees Sally every day. She and the Drapers have many aquaintances in common and live in close proximity. The affair could easily be discovered and destroy Don's family. Entering into it is a self-destructive action; Don knows it will likely cause him to suffer. This draws him.

DON'S MASOCHISM

As is the case with Suzanne, Don mostly acts out his aggression on himself by behaving in self-defeating ways such as drinking until passing out, and destroying his romantic relationships. And when Don calls a prostitute, it also reveals a great deal about the self-defeating nature of his personality. His date with her can be seen as an exercise in what psychoanalysts refer to as sadomasochism, or a pattern of self-sabotaging behaviors and choices. Sadomasochism was historically a sexual practice that involved pleasure and release in the experience and the inflicting of torture and pain—the masochistic individual both inflicted the torture and enjoyed having the torture inflicted on him; he took pleasure in experiencing pain, and in the tension he felt waiting to be punished as well as in the release of this tension. Today sadomasochism is generally understood to encompass all behaviors that involve cruelty and inflicting torture and pain (i.e., sadism), or are chronically self-defeating in nature (masochism).[4]

Back to Don. He seeks out women when he is lonely and wanting affection. He also likes dominance and control. This is clear. But why would he want to get slapped? Is he also seeking to be dominated, and is this realistic? In a word: yes.

Freud wrote about people who enjoy pain and beatings. Although the reasons for this are quite complicated, such individuals derive satisfaction and gratification from being punished, as well as from imagining themselves as the punisher.[5] Punishment and pain feel pleasurable, exciting. Deep down, sadomasochists like Don often feel damaged. They believe they deserve to suffer and get a thrill from punishment—real or imagined. Some have fantasies of being beaten or of beating others. The idea of inflicting and receiving pain is equally thrilling and exciting to them. A person who struggles with this type of personality can be seen as having fused both his or her sexual and aggressive impulses and his or her dilemmas about them—in conflict, he or she wishes to play out sexually exciting feelings with others, as well as to exert aggression on them.

Don's aggressive behavior and the way he uses people for his own designs mask his deep-seated feelings of insecurity and inadequacy. His self-esteem is low to begin with, and after he loses Betty and the kids, it bottoms out. When Don begins to feel this way, he unconsciously turns the situation around and causes others pain, a pattern he repeats with his wife, lovers, and his younger half brother, Adam. Don's calling a prostitute and asking to be hit are defensive maneuvers he unconsciously employs to protect himself from feeling small, powerless, and alone. *He* calls the prostitute. *He* asks to be slapped. *He* has mastered a situation. Instead of feeling lonely and out of control, he is powerful and in control of the course of events—and his feelings. When Don climaxes, he likely feels a mixture of pleasure and pain, tension, and relief. He enjoys the pain and the subsequent reduction of suffering when it is removed.

Freud wrote, "Masochism creates a temptation to perform sinful actions to provoke punishment (from the power of Destiny, a projection of the [conscience] into the outside world). The masochist must do what is inexpedient, must act against his own interest."[6] As mentioned, those like Don who engage in sadomasochistic behaviors believe deep down that they deserve to be punished and to suffer—and so they provoke punishment through acts that they view as bad or sinful. So, Don's getting smacked by a prostitute (Season 4, Episode 1, "Public Relations") represents what he believes to be his just desserts. And this experience causes him to feel in control because he has brought it about. In other words, he cannot allow someone he does not control to punish him, so he orchestrates a situation in which he controls the punishment, the pain, and the subsequent removal of both. Though he attempts to control his punishment, this often backfires and he winds up suffering in ways he has not consciously expected to each time his aggressive actions cause a woman he cares for to abandon him—his ploy for control does not always succeed.

Self-defeating behaviors seem counterintuitive; who would actually want to suffer? Sometimes the sufferer may know he or she has brought the pain upon himself or herself, and may even feel ashamed of doing so. Other times the sufferer has inflicted suffering upon himself or herself by making poor choices and repeating old self-defeating patterns because deep down he or she feels she deserves punishment.

Whether or not they are aware, those who self-sabotage often do it because of strong feelings of guilt, and a deep sense that they are unlovable and unworthy. Some may even imagine themselves being hurt or beaten—though no physical beatings have actually occurred; rather, these individuals have a sort of regular daydream about succumbing to what they perceive to be "deserved" imagined beatings.

Why defeat your own conscious aims? Why feel you deserve punishment? While there are many reasons for why some engage in long-standing patterns of self-defeating behaviors, there are some common threads to them all. Sometimes holding onto a bad relationship represents a desperate attempt to hold onto a parent, even a bad one. For some, it's better to be psychologically beaten than left alone or neglected.

Self-sabotage could also represent an individual's attempt to *control and master* old traumatic situations by bringing about pain in the present. While this sounds counterintuitive, it makes sense—the devil you know (and manipulate) is less terrifying and threatening than the one you don't. Though a self-inflicted loss causes you to feel pain, it might be preferable to know what to expect—that way you feel less helpless. So for many, the illusion of control allows them to tolerate the pain they have self-inflicted and believe they deserve, and to evade an unknown situation they fear would be worse. In other words, if a parent left you in the past, you might hook up with a serial cheater and unwittingly provoke him to leave you in the present.

Don provokes abandonment with Rachel, with whom he shares a deep connection. He does not get as close to any of the other women he romances. Though he asks Midge to run away with him to Paris and jokes half seriously about marriage, their bond does not feel as intense, and he has not told her about his past, as he has with Rachel and later Faye. Mostly he keeps an emotional distance from the women he beds.

Don's hiring a prostitute is especially interesting; it allows him to repeat an old loss and simultaneously experience a new one. Don's mother was a prostitute. He never knew her; she died in childbirth. Calling a professional for sex could be seen as an attempt to search for the mother he never knew and longed for as a boy. He unconsciously wants to bring her back; yet a lady for hire is by definition limited in her availability. It is inevitable she will leave. This built-in limitation ensures that even as he tries to reconnect with his mother he will necessarily lose her—prostitutes in this way become the perfect stand-in for his lost mother. Limited in time and availability, they are impermanent and will never be close to Don, a perfect repetition of the tragic circumstances of his mother's unavailability due to her early death.

Don's pattern of unwittingly driving away those he loves is clear. On one occasion Don's back is to the wall. After learning Pete has threatened to expose his fake identity, Don feels furious desperate, and trapped. He rushes over to Rachel's office in a panic and begs her to run away with him to California. Don's attachment to Rachel is deep. He has shared painful aspects of his past with her, things he never told anyone before: "My mother was a prostitute." He has revealed one of his most closely guarded secrets, and in so doing, has allowed himself to be vulnerable with Rachel. By asking her to flee reality, he has shown her the parts of himself he despises; specifically, his desperation and cowardice. His inability to face his problems is, in the end, what drives Rachel away.

People have an individual vision of themselves, their place in the world. They have an expectation of life and their place in it. They have what are known to psychologists as "unconscious fantasies," personal stories and narratives they weave for themselves—consciously and unconsciously—about who they are and what their place is in the world, as well as what their role and behavior will be in their relationships. Often such imaginings are not known to the conscious mind and, as a result, the fantasies get acted upon. Don simultaneously craves closeness but mistrusts people. He pushes them away, even as he deeply longs for them. In layman's terms, he fears engaging in intimate entanglements. Psychoanalysts understand such behaviors to be masochistic or self-defeating in nature. Pop psychology says that those who display this pattern of behavior suffer from "abandonment issues."

As we have seen, losing both his parents at a young age has made Don feel like his life and the world are out of control. His unconscious understanding of the world is that it is a lonely, rejecting place—on a deeper level, he believes he will be left alone, despite all his best efforts to find love. His loneliness and fear of abandonment elicit great terror and anxiety, which he tries to combat by unconsciously manipulating the people around him. In a strange twist, Don's fear of abandonment drives him to act in off-putting, cruel, or rejecting ways that ultimately cause those he loves to leave him. Commonly referred to as self-fulfilling prophesy, psychoanalysts understand self-defeating behaviors as a manifestation of masochism—a belief that one deserves to be punished and suffer, coupled with the excitement and pleasure one takes in the resulting pain and suffering, and in the subsequent reduction of the pain that has been inflicted.

Self-defeating behavior allows Don to feel in control, but it also brings about the loneliness he fears. By repeatedly provoking abandonment by Betty, Rachel, his other mistresses, and his brother, Adam, who hangs himself, Don can feel—albeit unconsciously—as if he is in control of the situation. His mind experiences some relief alongside the heartache of loneliness.

Self-defeating behaviors also represent an attempt to exert control when one feels out of control. Exerting control—even if it brings about a self-destructive outcome—creates the illusion that one is in charge and powerful; it is a way to master or bind the anxiety a self-defeating person feels when not in control of a situation.

As we know, control is very important to Don. He tells Bethany, Jane Sterling's college friend whom he dates, just how much he is willing to give and just how fast—or slow—he is willing to go. With Bethany, he is turned off by her assertiveness and efforts to take control (she unzips his pants and performs oral sex). She lets him know she wants a relationship. He chooses not to call her because he does not want momentum to build. He is repelled by her studied efforts to seduce him. In this way her plotting and attention to image reminds him of Betty's emphasis on appearances above all. And her plotting feels controlling. Likewise with Faye. After a romantic dinner, they are in the backseat of a taxi. He offers to drop her off uptown. They kiss passionately all the way there. When they arrive at her apartment, she invites him in, though she has repeatedly held him in abeyance during the preceding months. Uncharacteristically, Don chooses not to go to her apartment and declines to take things further. "That's as far as I can go right now," he says (Season 4, Episode 8, "The Summer Man"). He keeps the brakes on with Faye—possibly because she is a psychologist who is emotionally available, which threatens him and takes him out of his comfort level. Don's relationship modus operandi appears to be control. While his continually provoking abandonment seems confusing, it is consistent with a need to control. He exerts control over others and briefly feels powerful and shored up. But Don's women leave him, and his feelings of vulnerability and brokenness return to haunt him yet again.

DOUBLE STANDARDS

Despite the fact that women—single and married—seemed to fall at Don's feet, society outwardly frowned upon those who had sex before marriage. Why buy the cow when you can get the milk for free? the mantra went (and goes). This was the era of "nice girls don't," after all, like Shirley Maclaine's character in the movie *The Apartment.* While men were free to indulge, women could not openly have premarital sex without being "ruined."

Some women tried to break out of this stereotype, though. Peggy does not want to be pigeonholed into an old-fashioned sex role. She seems ambivalent about marriage. Despite Freddy's counsel not to have sex with Mark, Peggy remains unsure about what to do, and what she wants. She decides to go all the way with him. Clearly, she is also rebelling against her staunchly Catholic upbringing and background and the strict social roles imposed on women; she has also had sex with Pete and Duck. She wants to forge her own path and to take opportunities for herself—even those that have traditionally been reserved for men.

Joan succeeds in breaking the stereotype, though. She uses birth control, sleeps around, and still lands a husband. But even as she guides him in his career, she cedes power in their relationship by letting him treat her as someone who should put his needs first—she serves him, supports him in his career, and allows him to make decisions for the family, as did most of the women of that time. Their relationship is not all black and white, though. Joan uses sex and sexuality to retain some power. Greg defers to her woman-of-the-world ways and knowledge of etiquette, and allows her to call all the shots when his superiors come to dinner. More important, she allows him to think she is pregnant with his baby. But Joan is limited in how much power she can garner, and in how far her powers can take her. On the other hand, while Greg relinquishes some power to Joan, he ultimately retains most of the control in their relationship. She jumps up from the table to serve him and views her marital role as a subservient one.

LIFE AFTER DIVORCE

After Don's separation he moves from the Westchester suburb of Ossining to the West Village neighborhood of Manhattan, an area that has traditionally been less conservative than others, including the suburbs and the Upper East Side, home to Pete and Trudy. He opts for a building full of singles. He seems to be trying to get as far away from the conventional life as possible.

Don doesn't seem happy in the Village, though. He looks around at the artists and beatniks, and he scoffs at them. He doesn't find this existence any more fulfilling. Taking his dissatisfaction into consideration, it makes sense that he selects the conservative and polished Megan, an educated, cultivated, and maternal woman with traditional values. It is as if his encounter with Midge, who is ravaged by years of abusing heroin, terrifies him. It seems clear to him that Midge has nothing. He gives her money out of pity, then seems to run as fast as he can in the opposite direction. He flees the Village for the safety offered by domestic life with Megan. If we've learned anything about Don, it is that he will soon be back to his old marital patterns before too long, though.

For Don, Betty, Roger, Pete, et al, marriage remains as much a part of the fabric of the show as booze, sex, and the advertising game.

8

Racism, Anti-Semitism, and Homophobia

Men and women of color are seldom seen in *Mad Men*; when they are, it is floating on the periphery of the show as maids, elevator operators, and bathroom attendants. In Don and Roger's day, few African-Americans had attained positions of power in U.S. corporations and in professional realms. Thurgood Marshall made it to the U.S. Supreme Court, but he was more the exception than the rule. Most who had managed to find work at law firms, in large corporations, or on Madison Avenue were either elevator operators or janitors. As a rule there was little or no color at firms like Sterling Cooper.

Racial tensions exploded throughout the south as African-Americans demanded equality in education, voting, jobs, and day-to-day life. And where southern activist groups had once been fractured and disjointed, many were finally united by a single cause. Thousands came together to protest the arrest of Rosa Parks, who had refused to give up her seat to a white passenger on a Montgomery bus. Martin Luther King's "I Have a Dream" speech was carried by all of the major networks. After many years of disunity, a cohesive movement for equality was finally underfoot—at least for the time being. By the end of the 1960s, The Civil Rights Act (notably Title 7) had passed, mandating equal and fair treatment for people of color.[1]

The same period of time was one of relative calm for the Jewish people in the United States.[2] After World War II and the horrors of the Holocaust, anti-Semitism seemed to go underground as many Jews moved to suburbs and became acculturated. American Jews owned businesses, and many had established themselves in diverse professions. Quotas barring entry to certain professions, jobs, and educational pursuits were removed. It became possible for increased numbers to become lawyers and doctors, and to serve on university faculties. Many prospered financially and began to blend in.

The gay rights movement also picked up steam after the now infamous Stonewall uprising in New York City in 1969. That cause, once limited to a small group of radical activists, entered into the mainstream. Gay men and women began to live more openly, their sexuality no longer something they were forced to hide. Conservatives continued to present opposition, though. And the behemoth American Medical Association still clung to the narrow and critical view that homosexuality was a disease. But by the end of the 1960s, attitudes began to change. "People began to appear in public as homosexuals, demanding respect. And the culture began to react to them."[3]

So it began to look as though the activism of the late 1960s had left its mark. School desegregation, discrimination on the basis of color, and workplace harassment were now against the law. Individuals got involved. Paul Kinsey boarded a bus with his African-American girlfriend, Sheila, to go register voters down south. And though she quickly broke up with him, he felt he had made a difference.

Betty seems to try to be nice to her housekeeper, Carla, but winds up making insensitive comments. She views her station as above Carla's, even as she relies on her to run the household and take care of the children. We see that she's also very close to her family's longtime African-American housekeeper, Viola, when she cries on her shoulder, grieving for her mother and her father's illness. Their conversations seem to reveal that she feels closer to this woman than to anyone—even Don or Henry.

Carla is kind to the Drapers, especially the children, but this does not matter to the adults; racism—subtle and overt—is everywhere in the Drapers' world. Grandpa Gene accuses Carla of stealing money from him. Likewise, Betty tells her son Bobby, "Carla works for me, not you" (Season 3, Episode 3, "My Old Kentucky Home"). And her comment reveals her worldview: Things exist in categories and hierarchies. You are either black or white; Betty occupies one place, and Carla another, though she is situated on a lower rung. Betty and Don live in one part of the county, and Carla somewhere else—and it is not just a financial thing. Their Ossining neighborhood is white, they are invited by friends to join an all-white country club (but they don't), and they work and interact with Caucasian people. The only people of color they encounter are housekeepers, janitors, and the busboy at Don's favorite watering hole. Segregation was a way of life for the Drapers and everyone else who lived during that time.

Even as Betty is ignorant and lacking in sensitivity about race relations, she is not overtly hostile to Carla. She is somewhat genteel in this way. Don's colleagues on Madison Avenue, on the other hand, seem to be lacking in gentility. One day, Ms. Blankenship announces that she won't be watching the much-anticipated Ali-Lister boxing match, "If I wanted to see two Negros fight, I'd throw a dollar bill out my window" (Season 4, Episode 7, "The Suitcase"). The men in the office also make comments about "Negros." Just as sexist remarks failed to raise eyebrows, racist statements went unnoticed and were not remarked upon. The movement advocating for politically correct attitudes and comportment would not come around for another fifty years or so.

Don is not a racist—in comparison to his contemporaries, anyway. This was clear from the first episode, when Don talks to an African-American busboy as if the man is a peer who can contribute information relevant to Don's campaign (Season 1, Episode 1, "Smoke Gets in Your Eyes").

Years later the civil rights movement is a major story on every TV and radio show. Don hears Martin Luther King's "I have a Dream" speech excerpted on the car radio early one morning while he drives to work. He is present in the world and aware of how it is changing around him.

Betty seems less so, perhaps as a result of her confined female position. One afternoon at the Draper house, Carla is watching television. As soon as she sees Betty, she turns the channel. Betty asks what she was watching, and Carla begins to cry. "It was a funeral service for the little girls in Birmingham."

"I hate to say this, but it's really made me wonder about civil rights. Maybe it's not supposed to happen." Carla looks like she wants to say something in response, but she doesn't (Season 3, Episode 9, "We Small Hours").

Betty thinks the difficulties of many Americans and people of color do not affect her. In her view, the civil rights movement is divorced from the rest of her life. When she holds a fund-raiser and Carla is taking all of the ladies' coats, they all congratulate themselves on not being backward like their southern counterparts, completely oblivious to Carla.

But while Betty and her friends come across as disengaged, Carla does not. She is hardworking, soft-spoken, and respectful. She is kind to the Draper children, and to Betty. It is Carla who holds the Draper house together. She is aware of what is going on in Betty's life and mind, even if Betty is oblivious to what is important to her.

Roger, like Betty, was also raised to be genteel. Despite this, he doesn't spend much time worrying about what others think. He even performs in blackface at his country club because he thinks this type of humor is funny (Season 3, Episode 3, "My Old Kentucky Home"). Clearly, Roger is not concerned about making social gaffes, though he does worry about his professional image and about keeping his clients happy. He seems to feel he can say and do whatever he wants, whenever he wants, by right of his birth.

Roger also dwells in a segregated world. The only African-Americans he encounters are those in service positions. He is not challenged to think about people with any sort of nuance—he is the boss and has been in a position of power and privilege throughout his life. He does not have to examine his constant stereotyping.

And indeed, Roger makes racist, sexist, and anti-Semitic comments to anyone who will listen. In some ways he's an equal-opportunity hater. But while Roger generally manages to limit his tasteless and off-color remarks to women, and perhaps gays and Jews, his real venom is reserved for the Japanese. At a pitch meeting with Honda motorcycle executives, for instance, Roger is overtly hostile when they lay out the rules for a contest, the winner of which will get the advertising work. "We beat you, and we'll beat you again, and we don't want any of your Japanese crap. So, Sayonara." Bert and the partners confront Roger after the meeting. He refuses to budge on his refusal to deal with Honda. "I made a pledge to a lot of men you will never meet not to do business with them" (Season 4, Episode 5, "The Chrysanthemum and the Sword").

Roger reacts so harshly to the Honda executives because he is threatened by the Japanese. As a World War II veteran, he stood on the other side of their cross fire. The war with Japan affected his life in a profound way, and threatened the status quo. Even the wealthy and privileged like Roger were not impervious to the realities of war. And no group presented as great a potential threat to the American way of life as the Japanese before and during the Second World War. As Roger saw it, they had killed Americans and had challenged our position as the leading world power—this left him filled with hatred and mistrust for them. In his eyes, their actions against our nation were unforgivable. He would never see the Japanese as anything other than the enemy who had tried to bring Americans down. Roger embraces ethnic distinctions and uses difference to keep himself in and others out; this is the nature of in-group, out-group categories, and goes a long way toward explaining his membership in an all-white and elitist country club. It behooves him and other members of the old guard to preserve the status quo and its differences and distinct barriers to entry. Since they are "in," they benefit from keeping others "out," whether it be from clubs, jobs, or restricted communities.

Roger is like Betty in this way. People fall into categories and fit into boxes based on external attributes like their skin color, country of origin, or gender. But the similarity ends there. On the surface he is thoughtless and insensitive—he even tells Peggy it's "cute" that she (a woman) has asserted herself by asking for her own office. For Roger, the status quo is comfortable—he sees no need to challenge his stereotypical thinking or stop his grouping by external attributes. Why shake things up? He is comfortable and content in his higher, privileged position. As long as he can remain on that perch, he does not see the need to examine nuances or question his time-honored, rigid hierarchies and categories. In addition to allowing him to maintain his position in the world, denigrating others allows Roger to bolster his self-esteem. It is as if he thinks: "They are lowly; I am above them." Actively preserving these distinctions in his own mind helps him to feel good about himself and to secure his place in the larger world.

Another social distinction for Roger: the Jewish people. Sterling Cooper's only Jewish employee works in the mailroom. The Israeli Tourism Bureau, which had traditionally used Jewish agencies, considers switching as society begins to open up, and schedules a meeting seeking to boost tourism. Roger inadvertently introduces one of the potential clients as "Urine," even though his name is the Hebrew Yoram. Whether due to anti-Semitism or ignorance, he clearly sees Jewish people as "the other" at this point in time. This does not last. Interestingly, in just four seasons of the show Roger goes from never hiring a Jew to marrying Jane, Don's gorgeous Jewish secretary. This quick change is symbolic of the rapid evolution of this ethnic group and its sometimes seamless integration into the rest of society.

In a similar fashion, Don meets and begins to interact with Jewish people who seek to engage the agency's services. It is clear that he is not anti-Semitic; rather, his attitudes about Israel and Judaism border on ignorance. He shows himself to be open-minded and eager to learn about the Jewish country and culture. He reads James Michener's *Exodus* somewhat addictively. He romances a Jewish woman (Rachel Menken). But when the time comes to spin a campaign, he still doesn't feel as if he understands the essence of Judaism, nor does he have a window into what makes the Jews different. So, he calls Rachel, who reluctantly meets him, but says she has little to offer. Hers is a different sort of prejudice: Jew on Jew. "I'm not that Jewish," she tells him (Season 1, Episode 6, "Babylon"). She views herself as different and possibly superior to the less wealthy Jewish masses who are less acculturated or who live in Israel. She is Americanized, sophisticated, and evolved, she feels. Rachel does not see herself as having much in common with the Jewish people in Michener's book, so she doesn't really answer Don's question.

Don has never knowingly encountered anyone of Jewish descent before Rachel; he has nothing overtly negative or critical to say about Jews. Don's lack of criticism seems to place him in the minority at Sterling Cooper, where negative stereotypes are prevalent. What passes for an open-minded attitude is actually more in keeping with Don's plastic identity. He changes to fit the situation; he doesn't identify himself with any particular group because his identity is more fluid and less solid than others'. Unlike Roger or Betty, he is not invested in perpetuating categories and distinctions, in-groups and out-groups. His survival has always depended on being able to cross over and blend in—not on preserving differences and in-group, out-group status.

Often Don feels like he is an outsider. Work and the workplace are his lifelines. He says as much: "Bringing in business is the key to your salary, your status, and your self-worth" (Season 1, Episode 13, "The Wheel"). This is what matters most; it allows him to survive blows to his self-esteem, and it is the sole way he defines himself. While Don eschews groups and cliques, he does align with Peggy—clearly a woman and not a member of the power set, she is an outsider like her boss. He forms an alliance with her after Pete threatens to expose his true identity to the other partners. Though not a joiner, and not one to identify with members of a particular social or ethnic affiliation, Don groups himself with someone else in this case, perhaps because he is inspired by her speech about good people getting hurt and bad people getting away with misdeeds, or perhaps because he just feels like there is safety in numbers. This type of shotgun alignment is similar to his quick decision to glom onto Megan when the future feels shaky at the end of Season 4.

In psychological terms, then, Don chooses to form subgroups with women, but not with men or others similar in ethnic background. Allegiances based solely on superficial attributes like ethnicity do not appeal because they do not confer safety for Don. He does not trust easily, but when he does it is always a woman, never a man—and it is never just based on someone's social status or ethnic background.

While Don appears to be tolerant but non-affiliative, and Roger makes insensitive comments and dwells in a protected and segregated world, Lane's father, Robert, exhibits more direct expressions of racism. He is hostile toward his son's African-American girlfriend, Toni. He refuses to have dinner with her and Lane. While we do not know what Robert is thinking, he appears to loathe his son for dating a person of color. In fact, he beats him with a cane and instructs him to return to London immediately to be with his wife and children. Why does Lane's father react the way he does when his son introduces him to Toni? Robert's rage and paranoia are projected onto her.

People hate in others what they fear or do not like in themselves. If they feel defective inside they turn it around, unconsciously, so that the danger is outside, in the environment or another. They try to get rid of aspects of the hated person and project them outward. At this moment the other is viewed as threatening or undesirable—and as someone to be avoided. Once the turnaround occurs, the racist is merely a victim who has found himself in a position of peril. Any ownership of anger or hatred is disavowed; the mistrust is perceived as warranted and justified. The attitude toward the other is one of disparagement and sometimes even paranoia.

Lane's father's racism seems also to reflect a superior attitude, more than a paranoid one. Such arrogant attitudes are often compensatory for perceived defects in oneself. Obviously he is full of hostility and aggression. He displaces or shifts his negative and angry feelings onto his son. And he physically attacks him.

Lane assumes his father's superior attitude has everything to do with race and he tells him so, even after being brutally beaten. What Lane fails to mention or realize, though, is that his father is a sadist and a bully.

Sadists are those who enjoy inflicting pain. Lane's father looks like he has no remorse after brutally beating his son. After knocking him to the ground with his cane, he steps on his son's hand for good measure. In effect, he kicks Lane when he is down—a behavior that is sadistic and cruel. Sadists often enjoy receiving beatings as well (as we saw in the section describing Don's being slapped by a prostitute). Some who act this way are doing so because they are identifying with an abuser in a process known as "identification with the aggressor." We know nothing of Robert's relationship with his father or how he was treated as a child, but watching him reject Lane's girlfriend and inflict pain needlessly, we can surmise that cruelty was involved.

But while African-Americans and Jews have experienced some or much discrimination and prejudice, one could argue that the era's treatment of gay and lesbian individuals is even worse.

SALVATORE ROMANO, THE CLOSET CASE

Sal is a decent, hardworking, talented, nice guy—and he lives a lie. When he does the riff on Ann-Margret's "Bye Bye Birdie" it is suddenly obvious to his wife that he is gay (Season 3, Episode 4, "The Arrangements"), and yet he continues to pretend day after day to be interested in women.

Sal cannot reveal who he is in the early part of the 1960s, a time when the prevailing consciousness sanctioned homophobia and the bashing of homosexuals, according to Dudley Clendenin and Adam Nagourney, authors of *Out for Good*, a history of the gay rights movement in America. They describe the flagrant mistreatment of gay individuals in Sal's day: at one gay hangout on Santa Monica Boulevard in Los Angeles in the 1950s, for example, the proprietor posted a prominent sign: FAGOTS [*sic*] STAY OUT. The sign, cruel and objectionable by today's standards, appeared in a placard in *Life* Magazine in the 1960s, and brought the restaurant owner a great deal of publicity.[4]

Gay bashing and closeting were the norm. A Gay Activists Alliance (GAA) made attempts to raise money and fight discrimination but took years to get off the ground. Most gay men and women suffered in silence, hid their true identities, and did not protest publicly. Discrimination was prevalent even in educated and professional groups, such as the American Psychiatric Association. Until the late 1970s, homosexuality was considered diagnosable, and an "illness." One paper published in 1962 by Dr. Irving Bieber of the New York Medical College concluded that homosexual men were the product of "weak fathers and smothering mothers." But gay men did not openly challenge such forms of prejudice. Their wall of silence began to change in 1969, however, when in a series of demonstrations involving large numbers of individuals protested police brutality that occurred during a raid at the Stonewall Inn, a gay bar in Greenwich Village, and again one month later in Washington Square Park.[5]

By 1973 psychiatrists began to put an end to discrimination based on sexual orientation. After much protest and several marches, gay activists got an audience with the American Psychiatric Association's Committee on Nomenclature. Following their urging and after study by drafters of the DSM—*Diagnostic and Statistical Manual of Mental Disorders*, the bible of diagnosis for mental health professionals—the DSM was changed to reflect modern notions of sexual orientation. Instead of calling homosexuality an illness, as they did in prior versions, the drafters of the 1973 edition added Sexual Orientation Disturbance and stated, "Homosexuality per se is a form of irregular sexual behavior and, with other forms of irregular sexual behavior that are not by themselves psychiatric disorders, are not listed in this nomenclature." The drafters still insisted on a qualifying provision: "This diagnostic category is distinguished from homosexuality, which by itself does not necessarily constitute a psychiatric disorder."[6]

Given the ethos of the larger society during the *Mad Men* era, when even doctors proclaimed gay individuals to be sick and in need of treatment, it is not surprising that in the early 1960s Sal keeps secrets and feels shame about his sexual orientation. Don's relationship with Sal might be interpreted as revealing an attitude of tolerance. In one scene in an early episode of the show, Don witnesses Sal getting romantic with a young bellman at a hotel. Don says nothing. Is he as open-minded and forward-thinking as he seems—or does he just respect a guy with a secret?

Despite Sal's discretion about his sexuality, Lucky Strike's Lee Garner Jr. gets him fired. Lee knows himself to be the firm's most important client. He likes to throw his weight around whenever he can. He is insecure because he could not be himself in front of his wealthy tobacco conglomerate owner of a father. He wanted to learn about filmmaking, he tells Sal, but his father wouldn't have it; Lee's job was to step in and learn the business. His interests or aptitudes did not matter.

Plus, Lee is a bully. Though he appears tough and acts in a menacing way, he is cowed by his father. Bullies are frequently aggressive because they feel afraid and insecure. Their bravado serves as a cover-up.

One evening when Lee and Sal work late, he makes a pass at Sal. Sal immediately rebuffs him, preferring not to mix work and pleasure. Lee does not do well with rejection. And he cannot let word of his move on another man get out, so he demands Sal's ouster.

Don complies with Lee's edict. While he had respected Sal's privacy, he no longer trusts his word after seeing Sal with a bellman in Baltimore. Don doesn't exactly throw himself under the bus to protect Sal, but he is no homophobe (more on this later).

Lee Garner Jr. is, though—and in the truest sense of the word. Homophobia is defined as a fear of gay people that borders on paranoia. It is generally understood to refer to someone who is threatened by and rejects gay people for their sexuality.

Psychologically, it is a complicated phenomenon. Lee's homophobia masks his feelings of revulsion and attraction. In his case, it is a paranoid response in which the hater turns the situation around in a split second, and automatically perceives the danger and threat as coming from outside—this type of projection is similar to what happens when a racist person becomes paranoid about another, as Robert did with Tony. So by splitting off his or her own rage and turning it around so the danger is seen as coming from the outside, a homophobic individual succeeds in convincing him-or herself that the other person (who is gay) poses a threat. But in reality, there is none—except in the mind and psychology of the homophobic person. The set of thoughts and reactions that occurs in this individual in response to the gay person is the problem; the mere existence of someone with a different sexual preference is not.

Homophobic individuals are full of hatred. The hating and angry parts are situated inside of them. When they feel interest in or an attraction to others of the same sex, it is too threatening to be acknowledged or owned. So, they immediately turn it around—it is the gay person who wants them and will make a move on them. In this scenario, it is all in their imagination, however; and the gay person is an innocent by-stander to another person's internal dilemma. The homophobic person's paranoia causes him to focus on the gay person, who has, in effect, done nothing but stand there, minding his own business.

This is what happens with Lee. Though he comes on to Sal, and though the attraction originates in him, Lee needs to disavow such feelings. He is embarrassed and angry about being rebuffed, and he loathes himself for his sexual feelings and predilections. So he takes out his rage on Sal. In this sense his homophobic behavior can be said to involve a "projection" of his own hatred; a turning of the aspects he fears in himself onto the outside.

Not all homophobes and gay bashers are themselves gay, of course. But Lee is attracted to men. Some men can act and think in homophobic ways as an attempt to deal with deep-seated feelings of inadequacy. Take the macho guy who deep down doesn't feel he measures up. He might project or cast his perceived weakness onto a gay person, and then bash that person as an attempt to deal with a hated aspect of himself; in this case a perceived weakness—it is as if he would despise in another the presence of any similar characteristics he possesses, and loathes, in himself.

Lee is not just a homophobic and angry individual who exploits his power at the agency, he is also a coward. He sees immediately that Harry is nervous, and that he appears to be a sycophant. He knows he can push Harry around because he sees him as someone who is not a threat. Sal, on the other hand, stands up to Lee. Sal has a good reputation. Lee sees him as a threat. After Lee crosses a line, Sal could turn *him* in. Sal is not afraid. So Lee has to get rid of Sal to preserve his reputation at the agency.

At around the same time, Peggy's friend Joyce, who works in the photo department at *Life* magazine, makes a move, nibbling Peggy's ear. Peggy says no; they can still be friends. And they are. Joyce introduces her to members of the Bohemian Greenwich Village community. They smoke pot with Joyce's friends, most of whom are artists and writers. Some have "radical" views about the deceptive nature of advertising and the unfair treatment of minorities. Though Peggy spends time with Joyce and her friends and considers their ideas, she remains rooted in her heterosexual life and advertising job. And though not much is known to Peggy about lesbians, Joyce's friendship is an interesting addition to her life, as it seems to provide a tiny window into at least one other aspect of the New York City counterculture that flourished during this era.

While Lee and Joyce are both gay, they are from different generations and act in very different ways when they are around people who do not prefer same-sex relationships. The younger Joyce is a product of her cohort's rebellious style. Lee is similar in age to Don, and is confined by the expectations of his affluent southern family. So, whereas Lee cannot be around Sal, Joyce has no problem with Peggy. She can be "out," but Sal has to hide who he is—even though his true sexuality is clear.

TOLERANT DON

Despite his comment to Sal of "you people" (Season 3, Episode 9, "Wee Small Hours"), Don doesn't really come across as a rabid homophobe. He looks the other way when Sal has an assignation with a bellhop in Baltimore. He does not care what Sal does—or whom he sleeps with—as long as the clients are happy. Once Lee Garner Jr. complains, though, Don does nothing to defend Sal. Don's reasons for shutting him out are not discriminatory, though. He puts the client relationship above all; a meal ticket is more important than espousing the ideal of tolerance.

With no discrimination laws in place at this time, Sal and others like him were powerless. Sadly, the homophobes, racists, and anti-Semites of the world were free to bully anyone who was different.

And while things have improved (some states have legalized same-sex marriages, for example), many gay and lesbian individuals continue to suffer discrimination, on the job and in their communities. Likewise, racism and anti-Semitism continue to exist in certain segments of our society. Though we have made strides toward achieving equality since the *Mad Men* era, many believe we have not come far enough.

Afterword

Watching *Mad Men* leads us to wonder: Can people ever live up to their own individual expectations? And what happens when—as with all of the characters and many of us—people's idea of what they think they should be does not jibe with the reality of how they really are? Are the notions of what we want to be and what we really are irreconcilable? Can we ever meet our ideals, especially when outward appearances and reality frequently differ from what we hope to achieve or how we think we should live?

Betty strives to maintain the perfect existence with a handsome husband, a beautiful home, and 2.2 children. She does not seem to enjoy her family much, but she thinks that she should have one. When Don shatters her ideal by cheating she quickly finds another man to perpetrate the myth of beautiful affluent suburban existence. But even then her confused and unhappy internal state does not match appearances—or with what we know of her personal ideals. She is not happy with Don, with her second husband, Henry, or when she is mothering. She does seem happy to model and to strike out a bit on her own. Sixties gender roles prohibit this, of course, and she has to settle for what could have been, just as her personal limitations preclude her from providing the emotional support her children need and enjoying close relationships with them. Betty's perfect suburban life never lives up to her hoped-for ideals.

Don too has a vision of how he should be. He starts out as an insecure, bordering on obsequious, fur salesman and makes himself into a polished successful adman. He nabs a trophy wife and buys a beautiful home. But like Betty's, his glamorous appearance differs from his psychic reality. He knows at times that his cheating has brought down their relationship. He wants to be a better father who is more available to his children. He writes in a journal and tries to swim and get healthy. But his hopes and dreams never get fully realized either. He achieves a patina of success but remains unhappy and prone to self-defeating behaviors and difficulties in relationships, despite his vows that he can and should do better.

Joan wants to be taken seriously and treated with respect at work. She wants people to know she is smart and she has it together. In her ideal world she would be a member of Harry Crane's media department, not just a glorified secretary—and she would not have to strut around and be sexy to get anywhere. But like Betty, Joan is bound by a rigid social hierarchy and, like both Drapers, she is limited by her own foibles. Deep down, Joan remains a schemer who manipulates situations to get what she cannot otherwise achieve. She'll have Roger's baby while married to Greg, and she'll have a modicum of power over the women at the agency, but she does not get to live according to her ideals in circumstances that are exactly as she would like.

Freud wrote about such dilemmas in his paper on narcissism. He described the idea of an ego ideal, the particular hope, dream, moral code, and set of imaginings and psychological fantasies possessed by every individual.[1] We all want to live according to our personal moral compass, for example, and we all see ourselves in our unique set of ways (as successful, beautiful, talented, ethical, kind, helpful, healthy, smart—whatever the particular permutation may be). But we are human, and in perpetual states of conflict between our own desires and our external realities and personal circumstances. Often the facts don't match the ideals, and we are shorter, older, less successful, less popular, less honest, less helpful than we would like to be. And individuals whose ego ideals do not match with their life circumstances become dissatisfied, miserable, and depressed. Freud thought the disparity between what an individual wanted to be and what he really was or ultimately could be was inevitably a part of being human. Don and the gang seem to follow in this tradition.

But it's not all just one big downer of failed hopes and dreams and inabilities to live up to expectations. Many people do work hard to change and some do succeed in realizing their ideals. Peggy and Pete come close to getting what they each want in life—at least for now. They try to learn from their mistakes and to mature, and both are well on the way to forging their own paths as part of a younger generation that has more choices and fewer restraints. Sally Draper's character also leaves us with hope. Though Betty is emotionally distant, she takes Henry's advice to get her daughter the help she needs and puts Sally in a child analysis (at least until she moves to Rye). Though just a tween girl, Sally provides an example of how individuals who work to understand their inner lives and their own ways of tripping themselves up can exert more control over their emotions and destinies, and put themselves on the path to achieving their ideal visions of themselves—a long and sometimes difficult road, but ultimately one worth taking.

NOTES

PREFACE

1. In their new book, *That Used to Be Us* (2011), Thomas L. Friedman and Michael Mandelbaum, experts on global affairs, discuss America's loss of ground to China since the Cold War, and its need to meet challenges in four realms, including: adapting to globalization and its many consequences (e.g., loss of American jobs); educating individuals and preparing them to keep up with innovations in information technology so as to remain competitive on a global scale; addressing government management of finances, soaring national debt, and budget deficits; and finally, managing rising energy consumption and climate threats.

2. Andy Warhol was a 1960s-era artist who was well known for his pop art creations and bon mots. Warhol coined the phrase "fifteen minutes of fame," but is cited here for his ideas on the media's effect on popular culture: Andy Warhol, (n.d.). BrainyQuote.com.

Retrieved October 14, 2011, from BrainyQuote.com Web site: www.brainyquote.com/quotes/quotes/a/andywarhol109668.html.

INTRODUCTION

1. In his book, *The Psychology of the Sopranos* (2002), Glen O. Gabbard, M.D., prominent psychoanalyst and expert on psychology and the media, takes a look at the popular TV show; he applies British analyst D. W. Winnicott's notion of "transitional space" (the mental space used by a child to develop the ability to fantasize, play, and create), to the adult who uses media to achieve similar ends, pp. 9–10.

CHAPTER 1: MEET THE CHARACTERS

1. Virginia Woolf, a twentieth-century writer whose eye for detail and ear for prose captured the female experience of her era, wrote *A Room of One's Own* in 1929; in it, several female characters struggle with the process and execution of writing, as well as with their own literary ambitions, and embody the subservient role of women, dearth of opportunities at the time, and paucity of successful female writers in the era. Quote appears on p. 69 of reprint edition (1999).

2. Sociologist Helena Z. Lopata's groundbreaking book, *Occupation: Housewife,* was published in 1971, after the author conducted a study of 571 Chicago-area women in an effort to learn about their attitudes toward female gender roles. Most espoused traditional views, such as the idea that a woman's primary goal was to be a good wife. Almost all of the women she interviewed

valued marriage and motherhood over career or outside pursuits. Quote appears p. 363.

3. Sigmund Freud's and Joseph Breuer's *Studies on Hysteria* (1893–5), represents the first major writing on the early practice of psychoanalysis, then known as "the talking cure." The method and techniques described reflect Freud's original belief that making the unconscious conscious cured individuals of psychological ailments; in this book he introduces his topographical model of mind (which contemplates layers of consciousness including: unconscious, conscious, and preconscious parts of the mind, some of which cannot be known due to repression), pp. 1–181, Standard Edition, vol. 2.

4. Freud's paper, "The Ego and the Id" (1923), represents one of his most important papers on metapsychology, as it introduces the currently accepted tripartite model of mind, known as the Structural Theory, in which all parts (id, ego, superego) are understood to contain conscious and unconscious aspects that are constantly in conflict with one another and within themselves. According to this theory, defenses ward off awareness of thoughts, feelings, ideas, impulses, drives, and memories, rendering them unconscious, and such defenses often occur unconsciously, as well. The introduction of this model coincides with Freud's realization that in order for individuals to arrive at the insights necessary for the reduction of psychic pain, it is necessary to make conscious both the psychological defenses and the aspects of mind that they were defending against, and not to uncover repressed mental contents, as previously thought. Freud's structural model replaced his earlier topographical model, pp. 13–66, Standard Edition, vol. 19.

5. See Hanna Segal's *Introduction to the Work of Melanic Klein* (1964) and Betty Joseph's paper, "Object Relations in Clinical Practice" (1988). Both address central tenets of Klein's theory, including her contribution that pathology and Oedipal strivings are formed during the earliest months of life, and occur as the result of early parent-child interactions. For further discussion on this topic, See Jay R. Greenberg and Stephen A. Mitchell's *Object Relations in Psychoanalytic Theory* (1983), the seminal text on relational theory, in which the authors note that the relational school ascribes to the central aspects of Klein's theory.

6. According to Greenberg and Mitchell's *Object Relations in Psychoanalytic Theory*, relationship and insight together are mutative; Freud's classical theory held that insight alone was the agent of psychological change.

7. For a discussion of interpersonal theory and practice, in comparison to classical theory and methods of analysis, see Edgar A. Levenson, M.D., "Whatever Happened to the Cat?—Interpersonal Perspectives on the Self" (1989); see also, Sheldon Itzkowitz Ph.D., "Discussion of Fiscalini's Coparticipant Inquiry," (2005), paper presented to the colloquium of the Interpersonal Orientation, New York University Postdoctoral Program in Psychotherapy and Psychoanalysis, May 6, 2005.

8. Heinz Kohut's *Analysis of the Self* (1971) represents his first major work on self psychology; in it he elaborates on ideas such as the fragmented and defective self and individuals' attempts to compensate.

CHAPTER 2: THE CULTURE OF NARCISSISM

1. See, e.g., Helena Z. Lopata, *Occupation: Housewife* (1971), pp. 174–175. As Juliet Schor, professor of sociology at Boston College and expert on issues pertaining to work and leisure, notes in *The Overworked American* (1992): in the years after the Second World War, middle class was in reach of more and more Americans, p. 78. Dr. David J. Rossman, a psychiatrist interviewed by Studs Terkel in *Hard Times: An Oral History of the Great Depression* (1970), also refers to the desire to live "how the better half lives," p. 81.

2. In *Hard Times*, Pulitzer Prize–winning journalist Studs Terkel's oral history of life during the Great Depression and years following, one prominent psychoanalyst, Dr. Rossman, discusses the era's changing ethos in respect to differences in the individual conscience, p. 81.

3. Ibid, pp. 195–6. Another esteemed psychoanalyst, Dr. Nathan Ackerman, offers his view on shifts in personal individual responsibility.

4. Christopher Lasch's book *The Culture of Narcissism* (1978) was groundbreaking in its discussion of the rise of this personality in contemporary society; it considered reasons on both cultural and individual levels behind the explosion of the disorder, especially those explained by deficits in parenting, and claimed that our culture had shifted so that looking inward was no longer valued by most Americans.

5. See Heinz Kohut's *The Analysis of the Self* (1971), in which he discusses the central aspects of his theory on narcissism, including

the constant threat of fragmentation to the self and the individual's attempts to compensate for broken and defective feelings.

6. See, e.g., *Hard Times.*

7. Lasch, *The Culture of Narcissism*, pp. 162–172.

8. *Diagnostic Manuel of Statistical and Mental Disorders* (4th ed.) presents diagnositic criteria for use by mental health professionals, hospitals, and insurance companies. Certain personality disorders such as narcissistic personality disorder are classified under "Cluster B," as they are characterized by similar emotional states, traits, and behaviors.

9. *D'Aulaires' Book of Greek Myths* (1962). The myth of Narcissus appears on p. 92.

10. Originally *je pense donc je suis* in French, and translated as, "I think, therefore I am," this statement refers to Descartes' idea that being able to think proves the existence of a mind. This appears in his *Discourse on Method and Meditations* (1960), p. 24.

11. Plato's cave allegory appears, beginning in section 7.514a of *The Republic* in Grube's translation, (1974), pp. 167–191.

12. According to philosopher Immanuel Kant's *Critique of Pure Reason,* Pluhar's translation (1987), there is no a priori reasoning. Therefore, the existence of "a thing as it is" cannot be known; all we can know is what we perceive, pp. 93–4.

13. Freud's paper "Mourning and Melancholia" (first written in 1915, not published until 1917) represents his major work on object loss, and includes one of his most famous quotes: "The shadow of the lost object fell upon the ego." This is widely understood to refer to the fact that individuals never give up important figures from the past; rather, they internalize and take them in as part of the self. Freud also discusses the differences between pathological mourning and depression in this paper.

14. See, e.g., Dr. Harold Blum's (2011) paper, "Masochism: Passionate Pain and Erotized Triumph," *Psychoanalytic Review*.

15. In Glen Elder Jr.'s *Children of the Great Depression* (1998), the author discusses the findings of Jean Macfarlane, director of the Berkely Guidance Study, pp. 320–321.

16. Ibid. See economist Staffan Linder's comments on the effect of scarcity versus excess, pp. 293–4.

17 Zeus myth appears on p. 34 of *D'Aulaires' Book of Greek Myths* (1962).

18. Lasch, *The Culture of Narcissism* (1978).

19. Heinz Kohut's concept of mirroring (self-object transference of mirroring and idealization), elaborated in *The Analysis of the Self* (1971), represents a major contribution to our understanding of the early parent-child relationship. He believed that parents needed to provide a necessary intersection of empathy and limit setting in order for healthy development to occur.

20. In Hannah Segal's *Introduction to the Work of Melanie Klein* (1964), the author explains central tenets of Klein's theory, including her notion that primitive affects such as rage, paranoia, and envy are split off and experienced by the individual as coming from outside of him or her.

CHAPTER 3: WORKING STIFFS

1. *The Female Eunuch* by Germaine Greer (1971) sets forth the nature of the female gender role and the limitations that bind it; she discusses social restrictions that persisted up and until the 1950s. The directives for secretaries were first published on July 20, 1969 in the *London Times* and are printed on pp. 120–1.

2. Helena Lopata's book *Occupation: Housewife* (1971) includes results of her 1960s sociological studies of attitudes of Chicago women; for findings, see p. 51.

3. Germaine Greer's discussion of masculine and feminine aspects of personality and behavior appears on pp. 71–2.

4. *D'Aulaires' Book of Greek Myths* (1962). The Oedipus myth appears on pp. 160–161.

5. Glen Elder Jr.'s *Children of the Great Depression* (1998) is a landmark lifetime study of this cohort; for a discussion of the difference between this generation and the one that followed, in terms of attitudes towards work, see pp. 189–191.

6. Ibid. A discussion of "intrinsic" (such as match between the person and the job, opportunities job affords for creativity) versus

"extrinsic" value of work (wages, availability of jobs and geographic factors) appears on pp. 189–190.

7. Ibid. Macfarlane's quote about the maturational value of hardship appears on p. 321.

CHAPTER 4: SEX, DRUGS, AND JOHNNIE WALKER

1. *The Big Book,* Alcoholics Anonymous 4th ed. (2001): Alcoholics Anonymous World Services. The bible for AA tells the story of founder Bill W. and others, and offers a history of the recovery movement.

2. Different aspects of addiction and recovery are discussed in Mooney, Eisenberg, and Eisenberg's *The Recovery Book* (1992), for individuals and families struggling with alcoholism and addictions.

3. Martin Booth's *Cannabis: A History* (2004) offers readers a detailed and rich historical description of both the use of this drug, and efforts at its legalization; quote appears p. 211.

CHAPTER 5: SEXISM AND MISOGENY

1. In *When Everything Changed: The Amazing Journey of American Women from 1960 to the Present* (2009), *New York Times* editor and writer Gail Collins conducts interviews and analyzes both the limited options open to women in the latter part of the 1900s, as well as how women's roles and opportunities have changed from the middle of the last century until now;

see pp. 11–12 for a discussion of the lack of role models and mentors.

2. Stephanie Coontz, prominent professor and historian, considers the impact of Friedan's *Feminine Mystique* (1963) and society's limitations on women's roles from the '50s to the modern day, in her book *A Strange Stirring: The Feminine Mystique and American Women at the Dawn of the 1960s* (2011); see pp. 61–2, 64.

3. For a discussion of the lack of women's rights during marriage and divorce, see Coontz, pp. 5–7.

4. For a discussion of the sexism of the medical profession, see Collins, p. 166.

5. See, e.g, Germaine Greer, *The Female Eunuch* (1971), a feminist treatise, for social roles that bound women. Quote appears on pp. 220–5.

6. In *The Interpretation of Dreams* (1900), Freud introduced the notion of identification with an aggressor, but did not give this phenomenon a name. His daughter, Anna Freud wrote *The Ego Mechanisms of Defense* (1937), a book in which she outlined the ego's defenses, naming "identification with the aggressor" for the first time. Sandor Ferenczi (1933) further elaborated on this defense in his paper "The Confusion of Tongues Between Adults and Children, the Language of Tenderness and of Passion," in M. Balint, Ed., *International Journal of Psychoanalysis* 30 (Whole Number 4) [(1949), the first English translation of the paper], a discussion of the relationship between victim and perpetrator of child abuse.

7. Melanie Klein's 1957 book *Envy and Gratitude* is her seminal work; in it she reconstructs the infant's fantasies (phantasies) and feelings about devouring the breast (or bottle) during feeding, and describes how the infant's own wishes to destroy the breast it envies are experienced as "persecutory anxiety," a fear of retaliation by those in the external world.

CHAPTER 6: FAMILY AND CHILD REARING

1. In *The Culture of Narcissism* (1978), author Christopher Lasch's discussion of parenting in current culture appears pp. 162–172.

2. Harry F. Harlow's book *From Learning to Love* (1986) represents a major contribution to our understanding of the mechanisms and nature of maternal love in rhesus monkeys, and was intended by the author to explain similar phenomena in human beings; discussion of results appears on p. 108.

3. Ibid. Harlow discusses research methods and specific findings on pp. 101–134; See also Gary Griffin and Harry Harlow's paper, "Effects of Three Months of Total Social Deprivation on Social Adjustment and Learning in the Rhesus Monkey" (1966).

4. Ibid. Harlow also looked at what occurred when a monkey who did not have adequate maternal care became a mother herself; see p. 283 for a discussion of abuse by such monkeys; see also pp. 281–294.

5. Wednesday Martin, Ph.D.'s book *Stepmonster* (2008) takes on the daunting task of explaining the psychological and emotional

challenges faced by stepmothers and "lumpy" families, so known because the children of each newly married adult have come together with their parent, stepparent, and stepsiblings.

6. Mary Ainsworth, et al, *Patterns of Attachment: A Psychological Study of the Strange Situation* (1978). Developmental psychologist Mary Ainsworth's landmark study gave us an understanding of attachment patterns (secure, avoidant, insecure); criteria and discussion appear pp. 59–63 and 125–131.

7. Ibid. P. 130.

CHAPTER 7: SEX, MARRIAGE AND THE POLITICS OF INFIDELITY

1. David Cotter, Department of Sociology, Union College; Paula England, Department of Sociology, Stamford University; and Joan Hermsen, Department of Sociology, University of Missouri, "Moms and Jobs: Trends in Mothers' Employment and Which Mothers Stay Home," Council on Contemporary Families, Briefing, May 10, 2007, http://www.contemporaryfamilies.org/search.html?q=david+cotter.

2. Bella DePaulo, Visiting Professor of Psychology, University of California Santa Barbara, "The Place of Singles in Society has Grown Dramatically over Decades," Council on Contemporary Families Fact Sheet on Unmarried and Single Americans, September, 20, 2009, http://www.contemporaryfamilies.org/search.html?q=single+mothers.

3. Steven Martin, Professor of Sociology, University of Maryland,

"Recent Changes in Fertility in the United States: What Do They Tell Us about Americans' Changing Families?" Council on Contemporary Families Briefing, February 11, 2008, http://www.contemporaryfamilies.org/search.html?q=steven+martin.

4. See, e.g., Harold Blum's paper "Masochism: Passionate Pain and Eroticized Triumph" (2011), in which the author, noted psychoanalyst and executive director of the Freud Archives, discusses both conscious and unconscious aspects of sadism and masochism and how these problems are viewed today. Specifically, he notes that the sadist tends to unconsciously identify with the masochist, while consciously perpetrating cruel acts that might cause him or her to wind up in jail, whereas the masochist unconsciously identifies with the sadist, while consciously perpetrating behaviors that are self-punishing in nature.

5. Sigmund Freud's paper "The Economic Problem of Masochism," written in 1924, discusses moral masochism (one of three types Freud describes); in this type the individual believes he or she deserves to be punished and engages in behaviors intended to bring about punishment and suffering. Standard Edition, volume 19, pp. 155–170.

6. Ibid. Freud's quote on the moral masochist appears on p. 169.

CHAPTER 8: RACISM AND HOMOPHOBIA

1. Stephan and Abigal Thernstrom's *America in Black and White,* a history of race relations and racism, discusses the initial disunity of civil rights, as well as how the movement came together and has changed over time. See pp. 107–113; 154; 179.

2. Arthur Hertzberg, author of *The Jews in America* (1989), discusses gains in certain realms after the Second World War, though noting on page 308 that promises of equality were not kept (pp. 306–8). Hasia Diner, author of *Jews in America* (1999), discusses their acculturation during 1950s and '60s, and draws a portrait in which American Jews lived in once segregated areas, saw educational quotas removed, and moved up in corporate jobs and the professions.

3. In *Out for Good* (1999), Dudley Clendenin and Adam Nagourney's history of gay rights in America, the authors depict how hard fought the battle for gay rights in America has been; quote appears on p. 12.

4. Ibid. The authors discuss a placard that was published in *Life* magazine; though offensive by today's standards, it nevertheless resulted in publicity for the tavern that posted it, p. 33.

5. Ibid. Clendenin and Nagourney describe the police brutality at a raid at the Stonewall Inn and at demonstrations thereafter, pp. 21–32.

6. Ibid. See Clendenin and Nagourney for a discussion of activism and attempts to strike the concept of homosexuality as a "disease" from DSM; classification persisted until 1973, see p. 215.

AFTERWORD

1. Sigmund Freud's 1914 paper "On Narcissism" describes his original views on this condition (for example, it includes early

ideas, since disputed, such as the notion that a baby is not interpersonally related for the first months of life). Notions of narcissism have since been more fully described by theorists like Kernberg and Kohut, but Freud's notion of the "ego ideal" remains a significant contribution to our understanding of the individual's sense of self and his human frailties. Standard Edition, vol. 14, pp. 73–102.

SELECTED BIBLIOGRAPHY

Ainsworth, Mary, Mary Biehar, Everett S. Water, and S. Wall. *Patterns of Attachment: A Psychological Study of the Strange Situation.* Hillsdale, NJ: Erlbaum Publishers, 1978.

Alcoholics Anonymous: The Story of How Many Thousands of Men and Women Have Recovered from Alcoholism, 4th ed. New York: Alcoholics Anonymous World Services, 2001.

Atwood, Margaret. *The Edible Woman.* Toronto: McClelland and Stewart, 1969.

Bertrand, Marianne, and Antoinette Shoar. "The Role of Family in Family Firms." *Journal of Economic Perspectives* 20, no. 2 (Spring 2006): 73–96.

Blum, Harold. "Masochism: Passionate Pain and Eroticized Triumph." *Psychoanalytic Review* 98 (2011): 155–170.

Booth, Martin. *Cannabis: A History.* New York: Thomas Dunne, 2004.

Clendinen, Dudley, and Adam Nagourney. *Out for Good: The Struggle to Build a Gay Rights Movement in America.* New York: Simon & Schuster, 1999.

Collins, Gail. *When Everything Changed: The Amazing Journey of American Women from 1960 to the Present.* New York: Back Bay Books, 2009.

Coontz, Stephanie. *A Strange Stirring: The Feminine Mystique and American Women at the Dawn of the 1960s.* New York: Basic Books, 2011.

De Beauvoir, Simone. *The Second Sex.* 1949. Reprint, New York: Knopf, 2010.

Descartes, René. *Discourse on Method and Meditations.* Translated by Laurence J. Lafleur. Indianapolis, Indiana: The Library of Liberal Arts, 1960.

Diagnostic and Statistical Manual of Mental Disorders (DSM), 4th ed. New York: American Psychiatric Association, 2004.

Diner, Hasia. *Jews in America.* New York: Oxford University Press, 1999.

D'Aulaires' Book of Greek Myths. New York: Doubleday, 1962.

Elder, Glen Jr. *Children of the Great Depression.* 1974. Reprint, New York: Westview Press, 1998.

Ferenczi, Sandor (1933). "The Confusion of Tongues Between Adults and Children: the Language of Tenderness and of Passion." M. Balint, ed. *International Journal of Psychoanalysis* 30, whole no. 4 (1949: the first English translation of the paper).

Freud, Anna (1937). "The Ego and the Mechanisms of Defense" in *The Writings of Anna Freud.* London: Hogarth Press and Institute of Psychoanalysis, revised U.S. edition, 1969 (UK, 1968).

Freud, Sigmund, and Joseph Breuer (1893–5). "Studies on Hysteria" in *The Standard Edition of the Complete Psychological Works of Sigmund Freud*, edited and translated by James Strachey, vol. 2, 1–181. London: Hogarth Press, 1953–1974.

Freud, S. (1900). "The Interpretation of Dreams." *Standard Edition,* vol. 4, 134–162; 320–4.

Freud, S. (1914). "Further Recommendations on the Technique of Psychoanalysis." *Standard Edition,* vol. 12, 145–156.

Freud, S. (1914). "On Narcissism." *Standard Edition,* vol. 14, 67–102.

Freud, S. (1917 [15]). "Mourning and Melancholia." *Standard Edition,* vol. 14, 238–260.

Freud, S. (1923). "The Ego and the Id." *Standard Edition,* vol. 19, 12–66.

Freud, S. (1924). "The Economic Problem of Masochism." *Standard Edition,* vol. 19, 159–170.

Friedan, Betty. *The Feminine Mystique.* (1963). Reprint, New York: W. W. Norton, 1997.

Friedman, Thomas L., and Michael Mandelbaum. *That Used to Be Us: How America Fell Behind in the World It Invented and How We Can Come Back.* New York: Farrar, Straus and Giroux, 2011.

Gabbard, Glen O., M.D., *The Psychology of the Sopranos.* New York: Basic Books, 2002.

Greenberg, Jay R., and Stephen A. Mitchell. *Object Relations in Psychoanalytic Theory.* Cambridge, MA: Harvard University Press, 1983.

Greer, Germaine. *The Female Eunuch.* New York: McGraw Hill, 1971.

Griffin, Gary A., and Harry F. Harlow. "Effects of Three Months of Total Social Deprivation on Social Adjustment and Learning in the Rhesus Monkey." *Child Development* 37, no. 3 (1966): 523–54.

Harlow, Harry F. *From Learning to Love.* New York: Praeger Publishers, 1986.

Hertzberg, Arthur. *The Jews in America.* New York: Oxford University Press, 1989.

Itzkowitz, Sheldon. "Discussion of Fiscalini's Coparticipant Inquiry." *Contemporary Psychoanalysis* 42 (2006): 453–462.

Joseph, Betty. "Object Relations in Clinical Practice." *Psychoanalytic Quarterly* 7, no. 4 (1988): 626–642.

Kant, Immanuel. *Critique of Pure Reason.* Translated by Werner S. Pluhar. Indianapolis: Hackett Publishing, 1987.

Klein, Melanie. *Envy and Gratitude: A Study of Unconscious Sources.* London: Tavistoch Publications, 1957.

Kohut, Heinz. *The Analysis of the Self: A Systematic Approach to the Psychoanalytic Treatment of Narcissistic Personality Disorders.* New York: International Universities Press, 1971.

Lasch, Christopher. *The Culture of Narcissism: American Life in an Age of Diminishing Expectations.* New York: W. W. Norton, 1978.

Levenson, Edgar A. "Whatever Happened to the Cat? Interpersonal Perspectives on the Self." *Contemporary Psychoanalysis* 25 (1989): 537-553.

Lopata, Helena Z. *Occupation: Housewife.* New York: Oxford University Press, 1971.

Martin, Wednesday. *Stepmonster.* New York: Harcourt Houghton Mifflin, 2008.

McWilliams, Nancy. *Psychoanalytic Diagnosis: Understanding Personality Structure in the Clinical Process.* New York: Guilford (1994).

Mooney, Al J., Arlene and Howard Eisenberg. *The Recovery Book.* New York: Workman Publishing, 1992.

Plato. *The Republic.* Translated by G.M.A. Grube. Indianapolis: Hackett Publishing, 1974.

Schor, Juliet. *The Overworked American: The Unexpected Decline of Leisure.* New York: Basic Books, 1992.

Segal, Hanna. *Introduction to the Work of Melanie Klein.* New York: Basic Books, 1964.

Terkel, Studs. *Hard Times: An Oral History of the Great Depression.* New York: Pantheon Books, 1970.

Thernstrom, Stephan, and Abigail Thernstrom. *America in Black and White: One Nation, Indivisible.* New York: Simon & Schuster, 1997.

Woolf, Virginia. *A Room of One's Own.* Thorndike, Maine: G. K. Hall/Harcourt Brace, 1999.

INDEX

Made in the USA
San Bernardino, CA
16 December 2015